Being In Time
A Post-Political Manifesto

GILAD ATZMON

SKYSCRAPERPUBLICATIONS

"We don't see things as they are, we see them as we are." – **Anaïs Nin**

Published by Skyscraper Publications Limited
20 Crab Tree Close, Bloxham, OX15 4SE
www.skyscraperpublications.com
First published 2017

Copyright (c) 2017 Gilad Atzmon

Cover design by Rebecca Lynch
Printed in the United Kingdom by Latitude

ISBN-13: 9781911072201

I would like to express my gratitude to Eve Mykytyn, Paul Eisen, Andy Simons and Harvie Branscomb who helped me edit this book. I also want to thank my family who supported my journey all along and of course, the many people who joined me along the years in the quest for truth and ethical thinking.
- Gilad Atzmon

Table of Contents

Publisher's preface

The creature 'Gilad Atzmon' is sometimes used as a bogeyman to frighten Jewish children, but he really does exist. He is known to one group of the population as a superlative jazz saxophonist and another as a fierce and controversial polemicist on issues of Jewish identity. In the current climate, criticism of the actions of 'the Jewish state' or major Jewish organisations or groupings, is painted as antisemitism almost regardless of the nature of those actions. Atzmon, himself an ex-Israeli and ex-Jew, has written in detail in his book, *The Wandering Who?,* about the nature of Jewish identity and how different it is from the monolithic picture we are presented by the major Jewish groups, and he analyses that topic in this new book, setting it in the context of the major political shifts of 2016, and helping to illuminate how such unexpected outcomes as the Brexit vote and the election of Donald Trump as US President came about.

Atzmon's conclusions are uncomfortable to read but they come from a sharp philosophical mind, an 'in depth' understanding of the topic, and many years of observation of Israel, Zionism, and Jewish identity. Whether or not they will stand the test of time, Atzmon's conclusions are soundly based on evidence, supported by copious references to Jewish writers and experts, and worthy to be considered seriously rather than dismissed unread.

Karl Sabbagh
Skyscraper Publications

Foreword by Cynthia McKinney

I suppose it was my fate to be the one to write these musings about Gilad Atzmon's latest book. "Why me?" I ask myself— as if I've ever shied away from anything "controversial" or uncomfortable. And Gilad Atzmon's thinking is both of these (but only because we have allowed ourselves to become bound by certain social conventions that Gilad explores in this sequel to his first book, *The Wandering Who?*). Atzmon's questions and his answers are both profound and fundamental. And so, therefore, I am attracted to Atzmon's boldness in asking the questions that no one else would dare to ask—even as he might be profoundly unsure of his answers. While I was reading *The Wandering Who?* I felt proud that Atzmon allowed me (and the rest of us who read it) to peer inside his consciousness as he was exploring deeply philosophical questions about himself and the world around him. And then, I got a chance to meet him. He was on tour playing his saxophone and talking about *The Wandering Who?* He came to Atlanta and I was there to greet and to meet him.

In 2011, the year *The Wandering Who?* was published, I was ready to read it. I had just been through my very public ordeal with being targeted by the Israel Lobby in the U.S.; in 2002, Ariel Sharon had even come to my home state of Georgia to gloat after my first dismissal from Congress and after my second booting from that not-so-highly-esteemed body, I was freed to float into post-political oblivion—the place where people who are not chosen go when the Zionists in control no longer want to be reminded of your existence.

In 2010, I set out by boat for Gaza, but was kidnapped by the Israelis and taken to Ramleh prison instead. And, as I admitted in Kuala Lumpur, I didn't even know, when I started my career in Congress, what a Zionist was. But because of the incessant U.S. wars in West Asia and North Africa, I was forced to find out. Little did I know at that time, that I would meet this man—hailing from an entirely different part of the world—rooted in entirely different realities—and that we would find each other in being and in Being. As he was strapping on the bombs painted with Jewish icons that I was protesting, Gilad and I were slowly making our ways toward each other—toward this moment. And so, I can't help but think of this foreword as the culmination of our Being in this time. So, I thank Atzmon for asking his profound questions and for making his astute observations that I believe can only relieve us of a cancer that if unchecked will devour our entire being. So now, what could I possibly mean?

Atzmon, unknowingly, provides an answer to *my* question. I travelled throughout the U.S.; I know prolific writers and thinkers; I know the most well-known political activists; I know the U.S. political class: but none among them has been able to (or maybe it's just not comfortable for them to contemplate this and) answer my singular question about the U.S. body politic. The question goes something like this:

The Pilgrims came to North America from Europe; without hesitation, they committed genocide against the indigenous peoples whom they found here; they stole not only African technology to build the South, they also stole the Africans themselves, and because of slavery and the Trans-Atlantic Slave Trade, a crime against humanity, they were able to build a vast and wealthy country, the U.S. The progeny of the Pilgrims then constructed an international political and economic order whose purpose today is to obstruct the sovereignty of the very peoples in the Americas, Africa, and Asia that they totally dominated in the past by outright violent conquest and colonization. The United States became the bulwark of European privilege; and wherever its fellow Europeans went, genocide was not far behind—the English in Australia and Africa; the Germans, French, Portuguese, Dutch in Africa; the Spaniards, Portuguese, Dutch in the Americas; France in Haiti—are but a few examples of the many available to mention. Europe and the U.S. became wealthy beyond belief because of this theft and pillage. The Five Eyes spying agreement is but a reflection of the reality of the "brotherhood" that produced the world structure as it is today. And yet, without a bullet being fired at you—their progeny, the descendants of the Pilgrims—you've lost almost total control of the apparatus of the U.S. state—and all of the international friendships and structures based on it; this has been a largely "invisible" coup. How could you let that happen?

Atzmon brilliantly answers my question because, while observing events from a distinctly different Being in time—perhaps it was even the multiverse—he was pondering similar questions, too. Atzmon not only gives us his interpretation of how this happened, he also tells us why it happened. Get ready for it. His answers are damning, but he does give us hope that The Real can prevail once we understand the central role that truth can play in the ultimate liberation of our Being in reality in Time.

Cynthia McKinney

Epilogue

Watching the American presidential election in the wee small hours of November 9th 2016, I learned that the Democratic Party candidate's aspirations were hanging by a thread. Hillary Clinton was hoping to be saved by Florida's 'Hispanic vote.' Actually, she was hoping that the Republican candidate, Donald Trump, had managed to upset enough Latinos to secure her election. Later, as the evening progressed, we learned that Clinton's chances to become the next president were dependent on yet another slice of the American population - the "independent women of Virginia." In fact, all through the night, on various TV news channels, pollsters were analysing the diminishing chances of the Democratic candidate in terms of her failure within different particular self-identifying or "Identitarian" sectors. This peculiar development, in which an American national party is dependent on group politics should be no surprise to us.

The 2016 American Presidential election revealed that America is divided into two camps: the Americans and the Identitarians. The Americans are those who see themselves primarily as American patriots. They are driven by rootedness and heritage. For them, the promise to make 'America great again' confirms that utopia is nostalgia and that the progressive and liberal offerings are nothing short of an ongoing disaster. The Identitarians, on the other hand, are those who subscribe to liberal and progressive politics. They see themselves primarily as LGBTQ, Latino, Black, Jewish, feminist and so on. Their bond with the American national or patriotic ethos is secondary and often even non-existent.

But the Identitarian agenda backfired. It was only a question of time before the so-called 'Whites', 'rednecks' 'deplorables' and 'reactionaries' grasped that their backs were against the wall and they too, started to act and think as an Identitarian political sector. For these folks, the American flag became their symbolic identifier as well as unifier.

Those of us who have critically examined the evolution of New Left, progressive, liberal and Identitarian politics were unsurprised by Donald Trump's success. Indeed, the defeat of the Remain camp in the UK Brexit poll had previously exposed a similar fatigue amongst British working people. But what is the nature of this fatigue?

Our urban financial quarters are now saturated with glass skyscrapers metaphorically designed to convey transparency as well as fragility. But when you stand close to these glass towers you realize that the wall in front of you is no window but a mirror. And when you attempt to peep in, all you see is yourself standing outside. This book is an attempt to grasp that sense, that 'post-political' condition of being left outside.

In the post-political neighbourhood in which we live, much of humanity has been reduced to serving the interests of big money, mammon and oligarchy, with Left and Right, those two familiar poles of politics as we have always understood them to be, now indistinguishable and irrelevant. The freedom to think openly and speak clearly are but nostalgic concepts. Our Western Liberal utopia has turned into an Orwellian dystopia.

This book will identify the cultural and ideological shifts that were supposed to liberate us but in the end, have led to the complete opposite. It will highlight the means and the mechanisms that have stolen from us our ability to think and to feel, to follow the rules of reason, and to act upon them. Though this book is critical of both Left and Right, a large part of the text focuses on and disapproves of contemporary 'Left leaning' ideologies and discourses. To be honest, I complain about the Left because I actually care about it. For one reason or another I do expect more from an ideological realm that claims adherence to universal ethics and the distribution of Justice.

The title of this book echoes Martin Heidegger's[1] monumental book *Being and Time* (1927). For Heidegger 'to be' is to 'be in time,' and metaphysics is the history of the forgetfulness of Being. To be in time in 2017 can be realised as a wakeup call, a struggle towards understanding the mechanism that shapes us and the world around us. *Being in Time* is an attempt to calibrate our human faculties and

---

1. Martin Heidegger (1889-1976) was a German philosopher and a seminal thinker in the Continental tradition and philosophical hermeneutics. He is widely acknowledged to be the most original and important continental philosopher of the 20th century.

senses in a universe that has morphed into hostile territory.

The book is roughly divided into two. It begins with a philosophical study of the post-political condition. It redefines the meaning of Left and Right, and re-examines the political struggle between the two. It then identifies the ideological and cultural elements that have led towards the collapse of the 'political' as we know it.

The second part of this book deals, not with Jews, but with Jewish political ideology and culture. American Jewish historian Yuri Slezkine (b. 1956) began his book, *The Jewish Century*, with a bold assertion: "The Modern Age is the Jewish Age - and we are all, to varying degrees, Jews." This second part of the book is consistent with Slezkine's metaphorical observation. My attempts to understand the intellectual and ideological shifts that have landed us where we are, have led me to conclude that it was, and still is Jewish secular, liberal, progressive revolutionary ideologies that play the major role in the post-political shift. This section will attempt to identify these Jewish ideologies and strategies.

For some time now, we the people who dwell on this planet, have been reduced to a mere audience to a devastating drama that tells the story of our own destruction. Despite all the liberal democratic promises, we are not players, but forgotten, voiceless subjects. The time to speak out is long overdue.

The Twilight Zone

"I've gotten some of my best light from bridges I've
burned." - **Don Henley**

Left & Right

From a humanist, philosophical and universal perspective, both Left and Right are ideologically ethical and universal. Both attempt to describe the human condition and both offer visions that maximize what they regard to be 'the human experience.'

Left and Right have been battling ideologically, politically and culturally for a long time. When one considers the enormous body of thought, critical ideas and positions that are presented from both the Left and Right perspectives, one may summarize the history of political thought in the second half of the 19th and most of the 20th century as a relentless struggle between these two rival visions.

But I offer a different view. I employ a theoretical outlook that looks at the world of politics from an alternative perspective, not limited to the Left/Right interplay. I examine these poles as complementary systems that mirror the nature of *homo sapiens*. I will analyse the exchange between 'the political' and 'the human,' in an attempt to grasp how the condition of people, humanity and humanism are reflected within a given political system and vice versa.

Traditional Left Ideology sets out a vision of how the world ought to be. The 'Left' view can be summed up as the belief that social justice is the primary requirement for improving the world, and this better future entails the pursuit of equality in various forms. The Left ideologist believes that it is universally both ethical and moral to attempt to approach equality in terms of civil rights and material wealth.

But if the Left focuses on 'what could be,' the Right focuses on 'what is.' If the Left operates where people could be, the Right operates where people 'are' or at least, where they believe themselves to be. The Right does not aim to change human social reality but rather to celebrate, and to even maximize it. The Right is also concerned with rootedness that is often nostalgic and even romanticised.

The Left yearns for equality, but for the Right, the human landscape is diverse and multi-layered, with inequality not just tolerated but accepted as part of the human condition, a natural part of our social, spiritual and material world. Accordingly, Right ideology encompasses a certain degree of biological determination and even Social Darwinism. It is enthralled by the powerful, and cruel, evolutionary principle of the 'survival of the fittest.' For the Right ideologue, it is the 'will to survive' and even to attain power that makes social interactions exciting. It is that very struggle that brings humanity and humanism to life.

So, the traditional debate between Right and Left can loosely be summarized as the tension between equality and reality. The Right ideologue argues that, while the Left's attempt to flatten the curve of human social reality in the name of equality may be ethically genuine and noble, it is nonetheless naive and erroneous.

Illusion vs Insomnia

Left ideology is like a dream. Aiming for what 'ought to be' rather than 'what is', it induces a level of utopian illusory detachment and depicts a phantasmal egalitarian world far removed from our abusive, oppressive and doomed reality. In this phantasmic future, people will just drift away from greed and gluttony, they will work less and learn to share, even to share that which they may not possess to start with.

This imaginary 'dream' helps explain why the (Western) Left ideology rarely appealed to the struggling classes, the masses who, consumed by the pursuit of bread and butter, were hardly going to be interested in utopian 'dreams' or futuristic social experiments. Bitten by the daily struggle and chased by existence, working people have never really subscribed to 'the revolution' usually because often they were just too busy working. This perhaps explains why so often it was the middle class agitators and bourgeois who became revolutionary icons. It was they who had access to that little bit extra to fund their revolutionary adventures.

The 'Left dream' is certainly appealing, perhaps a bit too appealing. Social justice, equality and even revolution may really be nothing but the addictive rush of effecting change and this is perhaps why hard-core Leftist agitators often find it impossible to wake from their social fantasy. They simply refuse to admit that reality has slipped from their grasp, preferring to remain in their cosy phantasmal universe, shielded by ghetto walls built of archaic terminology and political correctness.

In fact, the more appealing and convincing the revolutionary fantasy is, the less its supporters are willing to face reality, assuming they're capable of doing so. This blindness helps explain why the Western ideological Left has failed on so many fronts. It was day-dreaming when the service economy was introduced, and it did not awaken when production and manufacturing were eviscerated. It yawned when it should have combatted corporate culture, big money and its worship, and it dozed when higher education became a luxury. The Left was certainly snoring noisily when, one after the other, its institutions were conquered by New Left Identitarian politics. So, rather than being a unifying force that could have made us all – workers, Black, women, Jews, gays etc. – into an unstoppable force in the battle against big capital, the Left became a divisionary factor, fighting amongst itself. But it wasn't really the ideologues' and activists' fault; the failure to adapt to reality is a flaw tragically embedded in the Left's very fantasised nature.

If I am right, it is these intrinsically idealistic and illusory characteristics that doom Left politics to failure. In short, that which makes the Left dream so appealing is also responsible for the Left being delusional and ineffectual. But how else could it be? How could such a utopian dream be sustained? I suspect that for Left politics to prevail, humanity would have to fly in the face of the human condition.

And what of the Right? If the Left appears doomed to failure, has the Right succeeded at all? As opposed to the 'dreamy' Left, the Right is consumed by reality and 'concretisation.' In the light of the globalized, brutal, hard capitalist world in which we live, traditionally conservative laissez-faire seems a naive, nostalgic, peaceful and even poetic thought.

While the Left sleeps, Right-wing insomnia has become a universal disease which has fuelled the new world order with its self-indulgence and greed. How can anyone sleep when there's money to be made? This was well understood by Martin Scorsese who, in his *The Wolf of Wall Street*, depicts an abusive culture of sex, cocaine and amphetamine consumption at the very heart of the American capitalist engine. Maybe such persistent greed can be only maintained by addled, drug-induced and over-stimulated brains.

Rejection of fantasy, commitment to the concrete (or shall we say, the search for 'being' or 'essence,') positions the Right alongside German philosophy. The German idealists' philosophical endeavour attempts to figure out the essence of things. From a German philosophical perspective, the question 'what is (the essence of) beauty?' is addressed by aesthetics. The question 'what is (the essence of) being?' is addressed by metaphysics. The questions: 'what are people, what is their true nature, root and destiny?' are often dealt with by Right-wing ideologists. It is possible that the deep affinity between Right ideology and German philosophy explains the spiritual and intellectual continuum between

German philosophy and German Fascism. It may also explain why Martin Heidegger, one of the most important philosophers in the last millennium, was, for a while at least, a National Socialist enthusiast.

The Right's obsession with the true nature of things may explain its inclination towards nostalgia on one hand and Darwinist ideologies on the other. Right ideology can be used to support expansionism and imperialism at one time, and isolationism and pacifism at another. Right ideology is occasionally in favour of immigration as good for business, yet can also take the opposite position, calling for protection of its own interests by sealing the borders. The Right can provide war with logos and can give oppression a dialectical as well as 'scientific' foundation. Sometimes, a conflict may be justified by 'growing demand' and 'expanding markets.' Other times, one race is chosen to need living space at the expense of another.

The Right is sceptical about the prospects for social mobility. For the Right thinker, the slave[2] is a slave because his subservient nature is determined biologically, psychologically or culturally. In the eyes of the Left, such views are 'anti-humanist' and unacceptable. The Left would counter this essentialist determinism with a wide range of environmental, materialist, cultural criticism and post-colonial studies that produce evidence that slaves do liberate themselves eventually. And the Right would challenge this belief by asking 'do they really?'

---

2. I refer here to the slave in an Hegelian metaphorical way rather than literally.

Liberal vs Literal Democracy

Just as our Left ideologist refuses to wake up, our Right-wing thinker will not 'switch off.' This dichotomy between the 'dream' and the 'real', 'utopia' and 'nostalgia', or between Night and Day may appear to be a recipe for never-ending turbulence and even disaster, but it has, for a long time, actually been functional and it was the complementary relationship between Left and Right that sustained the endeavour at the heart of political exchange.

This interplay between 'night' and 'day' is a mirror image of the human condition – the crude collision between the fantasy and the concrete, between 'being' (Right) and 'becoming' (Left), or nostalgia and fantasy. We shift between 'being' (what we are) and 'becoming' (what we wish to be). We wander between the past and its memories of rootedness, and the hope for change. The interaction between Left and Right replicates the human psychological interplay between the dream and the real, the night and the day, and also between Utopia and nostalgia.

I suggest that instead of looking at the world through the rigid lens of the Right/Left dichotomy, or a particular ideological perspective, it is more instructive to impose an alternative (meta-ideological) method that juxtaposes 'the human', i.e. the human condition, with the political spectrum as a whole. Instead of imposing any particular ideology, be it Right, Left, Marxism, Capitalism, Liberalism, Fascism and so on, I examine the complementarity between a political system and the human condition.

Let's test the utility of the above methodology using the post-war Western liberal democratic era. That is, the spiritually, culturally, technologically and materially prosperous years between the end of World War II and the collapse of the USSR.

The liberal democratic era was a vibrant phase in the interplay between 'the political' and 'the human.' It was fuelled by hope. Symptomatic of the liberal democratic era was the belief that people can alter their circumstances. Mistakes occurred, nothing was remotely perfect; yet, it was commonly believed that the means of creating a better world were somehow 'embedded within the system,' i.e. the liberal democratic system.

Liberal democracy didn't provide 'answers.' It was not a premeditated ideological apparatus, instead it was a medium in which ideologies and practices battled one another. It provided a template of vibrant exchange that facilitated a healthy correspondence between the political system and the human subject. Yet, there was a deep metaphysical substance in liberal democracy that transcended the mere exchange between 'the political' and 'the human.'

Mankind hovers between Night and Day, torn between the dream and the concrete. Human existence is a chasm; a craving for recognition opposed by reality. At night, I may dream of myself as wealthy and athletic, yet in the morning, in front of the mirror, there's chubby, impoverished me.

The collision between reality and fantasy is where existence comes to realise itself as a void, as a lack, where the real self is unattainable. The same applies to liberal democracy. It is a system that is mysterious to itself. It is where the political exchange takes place, where the Left dream meets its counterpart, the Right's concretization.

People who were born in the 1960s and before are often nostalgic about the 1960s and 1970s, the promises and beliefs that things were getting better. Barack Obama's first election campaign was, in that respect, a nostalgic moment. It was an instant of delusional liberal democratic reawakening. The recent surge in popularity of Bernie Sanders in the US and Jeremy Corbyn in Britain, both old-style Leftists, shows the same longing for the 'political era.' And, in fact, the incredible presidential victory of Donald Trump may not be much different; it evokes nostalgia of true rebellious freedom as opposed to the post-political tyranny of political correctness. Sanders, Trump and Corbyn have been reminding many of what the electorate's hope was all about.

It didn't take long for Americans to grasp that 'Obama the symbol' – the impeccable, visionary speaker, the inspiring, spiritual landmark – was very different from 'Obama the president', a calculating politician struggling to survive the onslaught of Neo-con lobbies and other self-interested oligarchs. Those amongst us who believed in the man held on to the hope that he could make the political reflect the human and *vice versa*. Those who voted for Trump will have to wait and see whether their new president can indeed make America great again.

The End of Fukuyama

In his 1992 book, *The End of History and the Last Man,* Francis Fukuyama suggested that the free market capitalism of the West was the end point of humanity's sociocultural evolution. Fukuyama was naive to contend that liberal democracy was the end of history. While Fukuyama correctly detected something promising in the system, he failed to identify methodologically what it was in the post-war capitalist miracle that made the Western subject hopeful.

A meticulous political scientist, but somewhat less of a philosopher, Fukuyama produced a model that was simplistic and left unexplained what it was at the core of liberal democracy that made it so promising. He didn't comprehend that it was the vagueness, the lack, the void, the unattainable at the heart of the liberal democratic political universe that mirrored the human condition (and the unconscious). He failed to see the metaphysical similarity between 'the human experience' and the liberal democratic political spectrum that transformed hope into an existential power struggle. This was the secret behind the short-lived success of the post war 'free capitalist' miracle. It was a promise never to stop progressing politically and economically.

Fukuyama has been proved wrong historically, philosophically and categorically. By the time he extolled the eternal nature of liberal democracy, the system had been dead for some time. Like the human condition it mirrored, it was destined to die.

The Post-Political condition is an era defined by a complete failure of politics (Left, Right and Centre) and 'grand ideological narratives.' Liberal democracy, Marxism, communism, capitalism, and free markets are all empty, hollow signifiers as far as contemporary reality is concerned.

Total detachment describes the current relationship between 'the political' and 'the human.' We Westerners are becoming keenly aware that we have been reduced to consumers. The present role of 'the political' is to facilitate consumption. Our elected politicians are subservient to oligarchs, major market forces, big monopolies, corporations, conglomerates, banks and some sinister lobbies.

Liberal democracy, that unique moment of mutual exchange between the human and the political, has failed to sustain itself. Fukuyama's prediction has proved false. Democracy operates to convey a false image of freedom of choice. It suggests that this dystopia in which we live is actually the crude materialization of our own (democratic) choices. Democratic freedom only conceals the fact the choice is illusory and generally meaningless or non-existent.

As we witness the demotion of the human from actor to mere shopper (defined by a symbolic chain of commodities), and as the political system drifts into an insular, self-serving entity, we have to acknowledge that not a single critical or political theory illuminates our disastrous social and political reality. None of our intellectual, philosophical or scientific models even attempt to depict the disastrous post political reality in which we live.

More worrying is that even the artists, the painters and the singers stay away. They are silent. A century of cultural industry and commodification of beauty have been totally effective in dismantling any form of poetic resistance.

Bye Bye Lenin

The Left has failed on too many fronts. In its struggle to sustain relevance, it wandered away from the working people and their politics, it completely failed to envisage a prospect for change, and surrendered to corporate culture. But the Right is just as dead. It was reduced to a crippled "counter-culture" as eulogized by the American conservative political commentator Pat Buchanan. Its stamina and principles were completely eroded by the intervention of newspeak jargon. While the Right may perpetrate wars and conflicts, without a true Left opposition the Right has become a meaningless notion. Beppe Grillo, the Italian comedian and the leader of the popular Five Stars Movement, explains the disintegration of Left-Right dichotomy: "They ask me" says Grillo, "'Are you on the Left?' I don't know" he answers, "I've stood still. It's all the others that have moved."

In sum, Left and Right lost all meaning a while ago. Today the terms refer to different forms of social clubbing, lingoes and dialects. Left and Right are now simply *forms of identification*.

At the time, British Prime Minister Tony Blair and his New Labour government managed to privatize every aspect of British life including hope; his right-wing American counterpart George Bush launched an immoral, interventionist, criminal war in the name of a fanciful liberation - a war which Blair joined enthusiastically. Both Blair and Bush employed the same general rationale – they justified a criminal, imperial war by referring to the 'liberation of the Iraqi people.' In 2003 no one remembered what Left and Right stood for. The difference between Left and Right had become meaningless.

For most of the last century, Western governments were primarily concerned with work and production. Politicians' popularity depended upon their perceived capacity to produce jobs, wealth, and the provision of education and health. Not anymore. For a while, governments were successful in maintaining steady consumption by means of credit deregulation but that is no longer the case. Until 2008 we obediently bought property and goods with money we believed to be ours. It has now become clear that we can no longer buy with money we never had and this realisation is due to the 'credit crunch.'

The Western fantasy of an ever-expanding economy has come to an end. We are becoming poorer by the day, while a few oligarchs triple their wealth monthly. For the first time in US history, children are poorer than their parents. We are shrinking, and, as more and more people are willing to admit, it feels very lonely down here and worse is ahead.

Fascism – A Transcendental Outlook

The 'political', as suggested earlier on, should be examined in reference to its ability to reflect the 'human.' Liberal democracy was a promising phase in human history because it was able to sustain the tension between the 'dream' and the 'concrete', the 'utopia' and 'nostalgia' that was embodied by the unresolved dispute between the Left and the Right. In other words, the constant morphing conditions intrinsic to free markets resemble the human condition, swerving between the phantasmic and the factual. It is this mirroring that made liberal democracy into a promising moment in the history of political thought.

Hard capitalism is, in some ways, a reflection of human greed. The call for a welfare state, commonly championed by progressives and liberals, can be understood as a political manifestation of guilt. What is it in socialism that mirrors the human? The simplest answer is a craving for justice; the ethical and universal sense humans share. However, socialism can also be defined in terms of greed. After all, it promises that neither you nor anyone else will possess more than I.

Juxtaposing the humane and the political creates space for a number of observations and insights that have been foreign to political and social sciences.

Liberal democracy was not the only political player in the last century. At least in Europe it had two ideological competitors: fascism and communism. When Francis Fukuyama compared the three political philosophies in the early 1990s he seemed to have been dazzled by the collapse of the Soviet bloc. He was convinced that liberalism had prevailed and would continue to do so, while communism and fascism were essentially extinct.

In retrospect, it is obvious that Fukuyama was categorically, historically and factually wrong. China, for instance, is by far more productive than the Western markets. The truth of the matter is that liberal democracy was already shattered by the time Fukuyama declared its victory. It had been replaced by a globalized, merciless, hard capitalist system that transformed the 'Political' into a careless, apathetic instrument subservient to big money and a few oligarchs.

Fascism, I believe, more than any other ideology, deserves our attention, as it was an attempt to integrate Left and Right; the 'dream' and the 'concrete' into a unified political system. Fascism was an incredible economic success, yet it failed to sustain itself. Why?

Fukuyama contended that fascism suffered from an internal contradiction: "Its very emphasis on militarism led it inevitably into a self-destructive conflict with the international system."[3] There is no doubt that Fukuyama is partially correct. Fascism was defeated on the battlefield in

3. Francis Fukuyama : End of History and the Last Man, pg 17

World War II, but this is insufficient as an argument against fascism as a political system. There are many other explanations for the outcome of that war. Would he have approved of fascism if it had survived the war?

Unlike communism and liberalism, "Fascism was not universal," Fukuyama claims. But this is not a coherent nor a winning argument either. First, it is not clear why a political system must be universal. There is nothing ethically wrong with a tribal apparatus as long as it is not celebrated at the expense of others. Jewish civilization, for instance, is inherently tribal and often hostile towards universal discourses, yet it has survived longer than any Western competitor. Second, some would say that fascism managed to develop its own vision of universalism. It was committed to the idea of 'socialism of one people.' It opposed 'cosmopolitanism' yet fascist regimes supported other local nationalist movements. German National Socialism, certainly the most radical form of fascism, even supported (for a while) the Jewish national project in, what was then, British Mandate Palestine.[4]

German National Socialism contained a eugenically-driven, radical intolerance towards minorities and the disabled. However, even that tendency – which most people now rightly regard as a brutal abuse without any possible

4. The Haavara Agreement was an agreement between the National Socialist German Government and the Zionist Federation of Germany and the Anglo Palestine Bank signed on 25 August 1933. The agreement was a major factor in making possible the immigration of approximately 60,000 German Jews to Palestine in the years 1933–1939.

humanist justification – was regarded at the time by National Socialists and millions of Germans as a genuine, legitimate and ethically driven attempt to bring out the best in Germans and to cleanse their race of weakness and so-called 'parasites.' In other words, as opposed to the enlightenment ethical ethos that made the human subject into a sacred entity, National Socialists believed in the primacy of the nation and viewed killing as an ethical move that could be justified in universal terms[5]. Although I obviously strongly disagree with this very problematic approach, I accept that in order to evaluate properly a political view or action in ethical and historical terms, we must examine it within the discourse in which it was proposed or practiced.[6]

According to Fukuyama, fascism was doomed to collapse. "If Hitler had emerged victorious, fascism would nonetheless lose its raison d'être in the peace of a universal empire where German nationhood could no longer be asserted through wars and conquest."[7]

It is unlikely that Fukuyama is correct here. We have to bear in mind that Judaic culture, which is dominated by

---

5. Germany wasn't alone at the time. Buck v. Bell (1927), is a decision of the United States Supreme Court, written by Justice Oliver Wendell Holmes, Jr., in which the Court ruled in favor of a state statute permitting compulsory sterilization of the unfit, including the intellectually disabled.

6. Similarly, the global mass slaughter of Muslims conducted by the English-speaking empire must be judged ethically and deconstructed within the neocon and Zionist mind frame that set that genocidal agenda. Time is ripe to ask, for instance, whether we managed to 'liberate' the Iraqi or the Afghani people?

7. Francis Fukuyama : End of History and the Last Man, - pg 17

exclusiveness and even animosity towards 'Goyim' (gentiles), has prevailed for hundreds of years in spite of countless holocausts. It is actually a dialectic of negation that maintains Jewishness and yet neither Italian fascism nor German National Socialism survived the war.

It may be possible that Fukuyama was misled by historical events and failed to grasp the philosophical meaning of fascist thought altogether. But he's not alone. In the post-WWII 'liberal' intellectual climate, it is politically impossible to examine fascism and 'National Socialism' from an impartial theoretical or philosophical perspective. Any attempt to deal with the topic is at best 'risky' and inevitably academically suicidal. Scholars and historians who attempted to do so have paid heavily for their actions.

Yet stifling honest examination of National Socialism has left open the question of whether the problems of global capitalism may be alleviated by combining socialism with nationalism.

The Real is Possible: Fellini vs Riefenstahl

A philosophical view of fascism is that it represents an attempt to integrate the 'ought to be' into the 'here and now.' It offers a 'third position' that attempts to synthesize Left and Right (equality and ownership) into a productive, nationalist, authoritarian political system that reflects a perception of the people's will. If the Left looks to change tomorrow and the Right is inspired by attachment to the history of the land, then fascism attempted to transcend the temporal – to meld the past to the future.

The meta-political outlook I offer in this book throws light on the issue. If liberal democracy offered a glimpse of hope because it reflected the duality between the 'dream' and the 'concrete,' fascism was destined to be a prophecy that fulfilled itself. Fascism was overwhelmingly popular and productive for a while because it managed to bridge the abyss between the 'fantasy' and the 'actual.' It was the political manifestation and materialization of a 'dream come true.' Hitler promised to make Germany great again. It was the concretization of the imaginary, but this is also exactly where it failed because manufacturing the Real is impossible.

French Psychoanalyst Jacques Lacan differentiates between 'the Real' and 'reality.' The Real refers to truth that is unchangeable and absolute. The Real is metaphysical and abstract. Reality, on the other hand, is based on sense perception and the material order. The Real emerges as that which is outside language, within the domain of the inexpressible. The Real resists symbolization, it cannot be reduced into a 'language game.' As such, the 'Real is impossible' because it cannot be integrated into a symbolic order.

Fascism was a political attempt to touch or even transcend into the Real, to bond the 'Political' with the innermost human by means of poeticism, aesthetic, the will and even irrationality. Fascism made people into God. It was doomed to fail.

Fellini's brilliant 1973 film *Amarcord* perfectly captures the essence of the contradiction. There is a magical vision of perfection when the *SS Rex*, the enormous, glamorous cruise liner and the pinnacle of fascist Italian technology, appears. The night is dark and foggy and the villagers are sleeping in their little fishing boats in the middle of the sea, waiting for the cruise liner to appear. When the liner emerges, the vision is captured from below, it invades the entire screen: enormous and magnificent. *Amarcord* is Fellini's nostalgic homage to Italy's fascist years: he portrays the spiritual unification between the people and the political in the light of the technological and industrial sublime. The people are small but the State's symbol is humongous. The magnificence of the State's apparatus elevates the people spiritually and physically. They are ecstatic and for a few seconds the Real seems within reach.

Fellini might have borrowed this cinematic language from the genius German National Socialist propaganda filmmaker Lena Riefenstahl. Hitler saw in Riefenstahl a director who could utilize Wagnerian aesthetics to produce an image of supremacy saturated with *Volkish* motifs, peppered with authentic German landscapes, young Aryan bodies and plenty of fire rituals.

Riefenstahl's work *Triumph des Willens* (*Triumph of the Will*), shot at the Nuremberg Rally in 1934, is widely regarded as among the most masterful propaganda films ever produced. But was Riefenstahl depicting an entirely fictional illusion? Weren't the German people an integral part of a collective spirit that was emerging around them? Weren't they an integral part of that rapid process of reincarnation?

The cinematic spectacle leaves no room for doubt, they,

or at least many of them, were full participants. In *Triumph of the Will*, the Germans could hear their *Führer* preaching ideology to their sons: "We want to be one people. And you, my youth, are to be this people, we want to see no more class division, we want to see one Reich." But Hitler can't just stop there. Such a change will demand participation and great sacrifice:

"You must be trained for it, we want our people to be obedient and you must practice obedience. We want our people to love peace, but also to be brave and..." The entire stadium erupts in excitement as the Leader pauses before he delivers his punch-line – *"be ready to die."*

"You must be peace loving and courageous at the same time, you must learn to suffer privation, without crumbling once. We will die but Germany will live on in you and when there is nothing left of us then you must hold the flag in your fists ... you are the flesh of our flesh and the blood of our blood and your young heads burn the same spirit that rules us ... before us Germany lies, in us Germany burns and behind us Germany follows."

The massive stadium is shouting and saluting, accepting their Leader's call for sacrifice. The Real seemed possible; in a collective spectacle, the young Germans and their spiritual guide touch the essence of Being. Did Hitler beg for legitimacy? He had no need to. Hitler doesn't ask for approval, he attempts to touch the Real. I am not sure whether any democratic or liberal system has ever achieved a level of support equal to the trust the Germans bestowed on Hitler, yet Hitler brought total disaster to Germany and

Europe. So the question is, why and how did fascism fail to deliver? Why did it drift away? Was it doomed to fail?

The answer is that in fascism's appeal were the causes of its failure. Fascism merged the Left egalitarian utopia with Right rootedness, mass production and private ownership. In theory, this should form a perfect bond, yet, it may be possible that the 'dream' and the 'concrete' cannot be integrated into a single political system. It is the desire that connects being and becoming, yet the desire is, in itself, within the realm of the void. It is mysterious and it cannot be materialised into a system. Fascism's attempt to touch the Real – its attempt to merge the fantasy and the factual murdered the desire: it was an attempt to make people into deities, and so promised the impossible.

In *Triumph of the Will*, the German masses are unified in looking up to their Führer. They remain beautiful and proud when the Führer stops preaching, turns around, leaves the podium and goes back to his seat. But Fellini gives us his vision of what happens next. The masses are elevated, they see themselves as the true spirit of the new Italian empire, they are integrated into the glory, they touch the Real but then, once the *Rex* fades into the darkness, the people quickly shrink back into reality.

They are a grotesque collective of people, of many shapes and shades, the fat, the blind, the lost and the last. Their inflated pride fizzles out with the departure of the *Rex* and they remain in the middle of the dark sea, small and insignificant again and thereafter. Fellini understands that the Real is impossible after all.

34

The Enemy Within

"The enemy is within, and within stays within, and we can't get out of within"– **Arthur Miller**

United States of Detachment

How did the political system manage to slip away? When did it become self-serving and aloof? When did we lose our ability to speak? When exactly did the exchange between the human and the political rupture? Why was academia silent when we were robbed of our most essential liberties? Why is it still silent? Why did the Left remain quiet when manufacturing was discarded? And why is the Left still paralyzed?

Since the late 1970s, two major political trends have changed the way we interact and interpret our social, cultural and political environments. One is political correctness, the other is identity politics. These two waves of thought, largely associated with New Left thinking, matured in the late 1980s into tidal waves that successfully obliterated a number of traditional and essential Western schools of thought. This transition eradicated the old, hegemonic powers; the church, family values, the cultural elite, but it also obliterated some elementary liberties at the core of Western culture. Both political correctness and identity politics have revolutionized the way we interact with each other and understand our surrounding reality. The results of these changes have not been positive. We have voluntarily extinguished our own ability to grasp the world around us. We are in a state of self-imposed detachment.

Capitalism, and hard capitalism in particular, are driven by the principle of the survival of the fittest. Social Darwinism is the body of thought dedicated to understanding this survival dynamic. And yet our academic, analytical and theoretical cosmos is subject to a tyranny of political correctness that is anti-Darwinist by nature. While Western corporate culture is guided by the principle of a strict hierarchy defined by the survival of the fittest, academia, media and culture suppress any attempt to grasp the meaning, the nature and the essence of 'fitness.' The following pages will delve into this sophisticated institutional oppression.

The Tyranny of Correctness

Political correctness presented itself as a noble endeavour to minimize any form of social, racial, sexual and religious offense. It promotes a greater tolerance and awareness of differences such as race, ethnicity, gender and physical/ mental disabilities.

Political correctness targets a certain type of vocabulary that could be categorized as essentialist generalisations (e.g., women are..., Jews do..., etc.). It promises to eliminate prejudices that are inherent to cultural, sexual, and racial stereotyping.

Yet, despite the well-meaning political agenda, political

correctness has proved to be a tyrannical project. The attempted elimination of essentialism, categorisation and generalisation has placed political correctness in opposition to human nature. The ability to think in essential terms, to generalise and to form categories is inherent to the human condition and to human survival.

In fact, philosophy is the art of essentialist thinking, it is the attempt to dig into the core of things in a categorical manner. Naturally, those who advocate political correctness are often at the forefront of the battle against philosophy and essentialism. They are basically leading the opposition to the Athenian spirit that is at the core of Western thinking.[8]

Even at its most innocuous, political correctness crudely interferes with freedom of speech, freedom of expression and most crucially, the freedom for authentic spontaneity that is at the root of poetic and creative thinking.

Political correctness can be understood as a 'political stand that doesn't allow political opposition.' This definition is often associated with tyranny but tyranny may be less dangerous than political correctness. Opposition to tyranny and dictatorship requires a rejection of a separate entity but political correctness is sustained by self-censorship.

In the long run, the social requirement to be politically correct contributes to the eradication of individual and authentic thinking. It operates like a Trojan Horse spyware that is planted in each of us. It starts to bleep as soon as we

---

8. It is pretty impossible to determine a categorical demarcation line that would define where 'correctness' becomes anti-essentialist, for categorical thinking is in itself an essentialist mode of thinking and therefore 'incorrect.'

delve into an authentic thought, it then shakes our operational system, we react in confusion and consequently we say things we don't believe but which just happen to be the 'correct' way to express ourselves in public. When X suggests to Y that Y is 'politically incorrect', X affirms that Y may be telling a truth, or at least is expressing a sincere opinion, but Y had better avoid this tendency in the future. Initially we don't say what we think; eventually we learn to say what we don't think.

I postulate that the most devastating aspect of political correctness is the manner in which it interferes with an authentic bond between the subject and the object. Political correctness proactively introduces a barrier that interferes with the manner in which we perceive the world around us, speak our mind, express ourselves and even feel. It plants shadows and black holes in the midst of our cognitive reality. The practice of political correctness employs intellectual shackling to re-shape humanity and humanism. It opposes the core of the Athenian search for truth within the Western intellectual ethos. Instead, we succumb to a Jerusalemite set of 'commandments' that tell us what is right and who is wrong. But for what do Jerusalem and Athens stand? We shall soon see.

However, it isn't just the philosopher who is interested in the essence of things. Scientific thinking also aspires to derive essential generalizations. The physicist, for instance, is intrigued by the general tendency of objects to fall. The biologist is interested in that which sustains life. The economist digs into essential patterns of production and consumption. And what about psychology, sociology and anthropology, those scientific domains that investigate essential behavioural patterns of different people, classes, communities and tribes, can these scholarly domains operate freely in an environment dominated by correctness?

And what about art and poetry? Is beauty not an attempt to capture the essence? Is the poetic not an effort to dig at the root of things? How many artists, poets and thinkers will we silence for hitting the truth, how many comedians will we ban (for being 'sexist,' 'racist,' etc.)? Political correctness curtails the core impetus of the Western spirit.

While Athens is associated with the idea that truth is discovered through reason, Jerusalem stands for the view that truth is delivered through revelation. Athens therefore, is the home to philosophy, 'logos' and science. Jerusalem, on the other hand, is the capital of law and obedience.

From a philosophical perspective, Jerusalem and Athens share no common methodology. The surrender to a regime of correctness is a surrender to Jerusalem. It is a strict divergence from Athens and its spirit.

1984

It is no surprise that the Left, committed to the idea of what the world 'ought to be,' installed correctness in the midst of the Western discourse. After all, it was designed to make our world a nicer place. But how, when and why did correctness become so pervasive?

Three years ago, I toured the US and Europe asking these

questions. My audience knew what I was talking about. Some confessed that they could never say what they think anymore. A few were genuine enough to admit that they don't remember what they really think. The older members of the audience could recall a time when they could think freely and intuitively but that precious ability had been taken away at a certain point. No one seemed to know how this had happened or whether there had been any strategy involved. The assault on our elementary freedom to think and express was a manipulative project.

Historically, the term 'political correctness' was used in the early-to-mid 20th century by Marxists and communists in reference to the Stalinist 'party line' as exacted by revolutionary commissars and other forms of thought police. The term was adopted later by the New Left in order to condemn and restrict sexist or racist conduct as 'politically incorrect.'

While political correctness settled into the Western discourse in the late 1970s, it took a while before anyone dared to analyse this phenomenon theoretically and critically. But in 1948, a striking British intellect predicted the emergence of the tyranny of correctness. George Orwell may have been the first to describe, in depth, the ideology and the theory that drives the demand for political correctness; in the novel it is at the heart of the Big Brother policy.

Orwell's prophetic masterpiece, *1984*, was interpreted for many years as a critical text on Stalinism and other forms of Red tyranny. But in fact, it was a uniquely observant depiction of the intrinsic intolerant tendencies that Orwell perceived in the British Left circles in which he moved. When I read Orwell's moving *Homage to Catalonia*, a memoir of his experience in the Spanish Civil War, I grasped that Orwell's experience as a combatant with the Yiddish-speaking International Brigade in 1936 had left him disgusted by the intolerant correctness that was intrinsic to the revolutionary-motivated warriors around him.

In 1949, soon after the publication of *1984* and just before he died, Orwell delivered his notorious 'Orwell's List' to the British Information Research Department, the anti-communist propaganda unit set up by Labour to counter communist infiltration. Orwell listed the names of notable Left writers and others he considered to be unsuitable as possible writers for the Department. Apparently, Orwell based his 1949 list on a private notebook he had maintained since the mid-1940s of possible 'fellow travellers' – members of the Communist Party, its agents and Stalinist sympathisers. I tend to believe that it was Orwell's experience in Spain that made him an opponent of the communist 'party line' and crude, 'red' dogmatism.

Furthermore, Orwell's personal history raises the probability that *1984* was a visionary critical analysis of Western Left tyrannical inclinations rather than a banal cold war Western depiction of Stalinist ideology. After all, Orwell set the novel in London for a reason. Orwell grasped prophetically that the fanatic obsession with the 'ought to be' would evolve into guardian culture which, rather than guarding the truth, guards the discourse, the language, the expressions and the metaphors. Rather than guarding ethical thinking, it will 'observe' possible truth-seekers, and keep them at bay.

Orwell's 'Newspeak' is a visionary description of the 'politically correct' culture to come. In his *1984*, Big Brother's domination is maintained by means of total control of the language and the role of the signifier and the syntax.

Interestingly, Orwell's 'Newspeak' was inspired by Judaic monotheistic exceptionalism: "What was required from a Party member was an outlook similar to that of the ancient Hebrew who knew, without knowing much else, that all nations other than his own worshiped 'false Gods.' He did not need to know what these gods were called, Baal, Osiris, Moloch, Ashtaroth and the like: probably the less he knew about them the better for his orthodoxy." [9]

Orwell critiqued the 'knowing without knowing,' the ability to plant knowledge that exceeds the realm of consciousness and sustains hegemony. The one who dominates the language, dominates the world. Consequently, the fictional universe of *1984* is diminished by constantly simplifying Newspeak vocabulary and grammar: "Newspeak, indeed, differed from almost all other languages in that its vocabulary grew smaller instead of larger every year." [10]

Those familiar with contemporary New Left political discourse are surely accustomed to the soundbite culture ('White male privilege', 'colonialism', 'fascism', 'apartheid' etc.) that has become the shrinking medium with which we

---

9. *1984*, George Orwell, pg 90
10. Ibid

communicate our reality. We are expected to adhere to a strict vocabulary that blinds and even mutilates our senses and critical faculties.

When the English-speaking empire launched its so-called War on Terror, bitter opponents and critical forces were entitled to criticize the 'imperialist, oil-driven,' and 'expansionist' governments that declared that war. Yet those who attempted to point at the clear, intensive Zionist lobbying at the heart of the Neo-Conservative school that pushed for the war were denounced as vile 'anti-Semites.' Those who pointed out that Israel supporter Lord Levy was the chief fundraiser for the Blair Government that took Britain into the war were silenced using the same method. Those who noted that it was David Aaronovitch and Nick Cohen, two *Jewish Chronicle* journalists, who openly advocated the war, were ostracized by the media and in particular by the *Guardian*. Interestingly enough, it wasn't the hardcore Zionist media that waged the campaign to obliterate elementary fact finding. It was the so-called 'progressive' and liberal networks and outlets that were recruited to define the exact parameters of correctness.

The Palestinian solidarity discourse is no different. Support for Palestine is restricted by rules of 'correctness' set to prevent any attempt to grasp the origin of the conflict or its true possible resolution.[11]

---

11. As it becomes obvious to a growing number of commentators, analysts and academics that, since Israel defines itself as the Jewish State, its airplanes are decorated with Jewish symbols and it is supported institutionally by Jewish lobbies around the world, then its Jewishness must be examined in

In his novel *1984*, Orwell understood that interference with language is nothing short of an attempt to limit intellectual freedom: "A person growing up with Newspeak as his sole language would no more know that equal had once had the secondary meaning of 'politically equal', or that free had once meant 'intellectually free.'"[12]

The *Guardian*, *Democracy Now*, the *Huffington Post* and other progressive and liberal outlets have gradually reduced their reporting into a broken jargon driven by a score of sound-bites. They sustain a sense of political exchange to hide the tragic fact that true political exchange was obliterated a long time ago.

The philosophical and ideological parallels between Orwellian Newspeak and political correctness are staggering. Both are orchestrated, institutional attempts to deviate from truthfulness, essentiality, authenticity and critical thinking. The task ahead of us is becoming clear. We must examine how 'correctness' is maintained and by whom.

---

order to understand Israel. Nevertheless, some of Israel's harshest critics continue to insist such an approach is utterly 'incorrect' and that the only legitimate criticism of the Jewish state must be aired in the context of Israel being 'colonialist' and an 'apartheid' apparatus. This is a crude attempt to dominate our comprehension of our universe by restricting the terminology.

12. *1984*, George Orwell, Appendix, The Principles of Newspeak

United Against Unity

What does it take, in an era dominated by progressive identity politics, to be accepted as a fully qualified member of the 'New Left' or to be considered a 'liberal?'

Jane is a well-off London lawyer who identifies politically 'as a woman,' and marches enthusiastically for human rights. Can she join? I think the answer is yes, she can.

George is a medical doctor who also happens to be a black man and identifies as 'Black middle class.' Can he subscribe to a progressive email group and contribute to the discussion? I hope and suspect that he can.

And what about Julie? She runs a real estate agency on the posh side of town but she also identifies politically as a 'gay lesbian,' can she join the parade? What a question! Of course she can.

Abe is an accountant and very attached to his Jewish heritage. Abe identifies as a 'secular liberal Jew,' can he join the anti-war movement? More than likely he can, in fact, he may even, within hours of his joining, find himself in a position of leadership.

But what about Hammed, a metal worker from Birmingham? Hammed identifies as a 'Muslim' – can he join a Left demonstration against the War in Syria? It's a good question and the answer is not immediately obvious because it's no secret that many of those who subscribe to 'progressive' and 'liberal' ideologies and especially activists, are rather troubled by religion in general and Islam in particular.

So, while Hammed identifies with an inclusive, universal and humanist precept, Jane, 'the woman', Julie 'the gay lesbian' and George 'the Black' subscribe to political identities that are largely determined by biology. Furthermore, Abe, as a secular Jew, affiliates himself with an (imaginary) blood-based ethnocentric tribal identity. Clearly, the contemporary so called 'New Left' has no problem with marginal and exclusivist political identities that are often biologically oriented.

How has the contemporary 'liberal' discourse been sustained by people who subscribe to biologically-determined identity politics, yet often reject those who actually support equality, human rights issues and who are also often from the working class? Could it be that the 'New Left' is detached from working class politics and instead focuses on a vague and inconsistent pseudo-empathic discourse primarily engaged in sectarian battles?

Let's consider some more possible cases:

Uri is an Israeli peace activist and writer who identifies as an Israeli Leftist. Is Uri welcome within the progressive network? The answer is an unreserved yes.

But how about John Smith, an English bus driver from

Liverpool who is proud to be English and 'as a patriotic Englishman' opposes the war because John truly believes that peace is patriotic. Can he join an anti-war protest and, while he's at it, carry a Union Jack to demonstrations? Perhaps.

Tony is a 'Jewish Socialist' – certainly not religious but an ethnic Jew who identifies 'as a Jew' racially and ethnically. And by the way, Tony also operates politically within Jews-only anti-Zionist groups. Tony is hugely welcome at most progressive gatherings. But can the same be said for Franz who identifies as an 'Aryan socialist?' I suspect not.

The point is that there is a critical discrepancy in contemporary Left, liberal and progressive movements between professed humanism and the reality on the ground. Jewish ethnocentrism and even Jewish racial exclusivity is fully accepted, while other forms of ethnocentrism are bluntly rejected.[13]

And, while we're at it, what about Laura? She's a Muslim convert who often hides her face behind a veil. Does she feel comfortable in 'progressive' or liberal gatherings? Not really. But Laura certainly supports human rights and equality almost as much as she loves Allah. But the Left, supposedly progressive and liberal, shows very little tolerance towards Allah worshippers while worshippers of the Talmud who are

---

13. Black ethnocentrism had been accepted within the progressive milieu for some time, however this has changed recently once it was revealed that Black Lives Matter stood for the Palestinians. To read more: http://www.theatlantic.com/politics/archive/2016/08/why-did-black-american-activists-start-caring-about-palestine/496088/

willing to oppose Israel are not only tolerated, they are welcomed. Torah Jews, for instance, are often invited to progressive gatherings though, it must be said, they may encounter some resentment, especially from Jewish secular activists (this surely is because progressive Jews don't like to be ethnically and 'racially' associated with 'reactionary' people in caftans).

Membership in a progressive club is not a straightforward matter. We are dealing with an operation that is far from being universal, open or inclusive. The discourse is selective, incoherent and unprincipled. The working class is not represented unless they demonstrate adherence to an Identitarian ideology and subscribe to a predetermined tablet of diverse 'correct politics', or shall we call it, an inconsistent set of progressive values. If they espouse a commitment to 'working class' values, its presence is not detectable.

So what are 'correct politics?' Where are they defined and by whom? Is it the same people who set a 'progressive threshold' that excludes the Muslim, the nationalist and the so-called 'White' (whatever that means), yet embraces biologically-determined sectarian politics and even racial categories?

The Identitarian Shift & the Primacy of the Symptom

As the almost millennium-old saying goes, 'The road to hell is paved with good intentions.' Like political correctness, identity (ID) politics is presented as a breath of fresh liberal and progressive air, an attempt to introduce an authentic, ethical, political discourse – a celebration of diversity and individuality. But in practice, ID politics accomplishes the complete opposite.

ID politics manifests itself as a set of group identification strategies. It subdues the 'I' in favour of symbolic identifiers: the ring on the appropriate ear, the nose stud, the type of skullcap, the colour of the scarf and so on.

Within the ID political cosmos, newly emerging 'tribes' (gays, lesbians, Jews, Blacks, vegans, etc.) are marched into the desert, led towards an appealing 'promised land', where the primacy of the symptom (gender, sexual orientation, ethnicity, skin colour etc.) is supposed to evolve into a world in itself. But the liberal utopia is in practice a sectarian and segregated amalgam of ghettos that are blind to each other. It has nothing in common with the promised universal, inclusive cosmos.

'The personal is political,' as the common feminists and liberal preachers have disseminated since the 1960s, is a phrase designed to disguise the obvious; the personal is actually the antithesis of the political. It is, in fact, the disparity between the personal and the political that makes humanism into an evolving exchange known as history. Within the Identitarian discourse, the so-called 'personal' replaces true and genuine individualism with phony group identification – it suppresses all sense of authenticity, rootedness and belonging, in favour of a symbolism and an imaginary collectivism that is supported by rituals and empty soundbites.

Why are we willing to subject ourselves to politics based on biology, and who wrote this new theology found in pamphlets and in the growing numbers of ID Studies textbooks? Is there a contemporaneous God? And who created the 'pillar of cloud' we are all to follow?

It is clear that elements within the New Left, together with Jewish progressive and liberal intelligentsia, have been at the heart of the formation of the ideological foundation of ID politics. At least traditionally, both Jewish liberals and the Left were associated with opposition to any form of exclusive political agenda based on biology or ethnicity. Yet, one may wonder why does the New Left espouse such an exclusivist, sectarian and biologically-driven agenda?

For the old, traditional, union-based Left, it was difficult to digest the fact that the proletarian subject was often patriotic, nationalist and unexcited by 'working-class politics.' The Left was pained when the worker failed to be convinced by the 'revolution' and revolutionary prospects. This tormenting paradox at the heart of Left politics can be easily understood – the people who claim to represent the worker are, most often, in a constant state of detachment from workers, their needs and whims. In short, it is hard for the Left to accept that the lower classes are often sympathetic to conservative politics and attached to traditional values.

Working class apathy towards the Left is understandable. The worker, the 'proletarian,' draws confidence and pride from the flag, nationalism and rootedness in his soil. National loyalty and rootedness make the British subject, for instance, an integral part of an empire and a glorious past. He or she is associated with a chain of scientific, technological, military and cultural achievements. It is the Union Jack that turns Newton, Nelson, Churchill and Shakespeare into extended family members.

For the lower classes, the flag is a symbol of belonging that offers a true sense of collective diversity – we are one, against all odds - in spite of socio-economic differences, in spite of the manifold of ethnicities and differences in culture, upbringing and education. Within the context of patriotic discourse, we are stuck here together in a muddy trench in the Somme or in a tank in El Alamein, just because we are truly one people after all.

This observation explains why, unlike the *Guardian* reader, working people are actually attached to the British royal family and even the aristocracy. This may help explain the popularity of Oswald Mosley and his British Union of Fascists in the 1930s. When Mosley, himself an aristocrat, was asked about his popularity amongst the working classes, he answered – "we were together in the trenches."

The same can be said about Nigel Farage and UKIP. The British workers who follow Farage are not bothered that Farage is a veteran city Mammonite. They see in him one of their own because (from a nationalist perspective) he is one of them.

In 2016, we learned that the American blue-collar workers dumped the Democratic candidate, Hillary Clinton and her 'progressive mantra' in favour of Republican multi-billionaire Donald Trump. Was this a coincidence? Not at all. Working people are often proudly nationalistic and patriotic. They are proud of their aristocracy and even align themselves with the rich and the elite. When Donald Trump Jr. was asked to explain his dad's popularity amongst workers his answer was straightforward. "I've always called him the blue-collar billionaire because that's what he is. He is able to talk to those people. He's not talking at them. He's talking with them."[14] The 2016 USA presidential election proves that Donald Jr. was spot on. Trump's support with white blue-collar workers secured his election.[15]

The traditional cosmopolitan Left lacks the political means to replace this rapturous sense of *volkish* belonging with anything meaningful or popular enough to compete. It is not that traditional Left ideology is wrong, it is just lacking. It has not managed to outshine the magnetic allure that is inherent in patriotism and rootedness. Thinkers such as George Sorel and Antonio Gramsci, who inspired Marxists, fascists and communists, grasped that the revolution won't be carried out by the proletariat alone. They believed that sophistication and cultural manipulation were essential. And they were right.

ID politics was intended to cure this systemic failure of the Left. It offers a new cosmopolitan spirit alongside a strong sense of belonging. Like Bolshevism, it offers a global

---

14. http://pittsburgh.cbslocal.com/2016/09/14/donald-trump-jr-refers-to-dad-a-the-blue-collar-billionaire-during-pittsburgh-campaign-stop/

15. Donald Trump support with blue-collar workers was within a 40% margin over democratic challenger Hillary Clinton. http://www.forbes.com/sites/daviddavenport/2016/11/15/voter-message-jobs-and-the-american-dream-trump-the-welfare-state/#1af7dd2637c3

template of political alliances that cross borders, oceans and continents. The biological element – skin colour, gender and sexual orientation - offers a vision of an international struggle that is ethically grounded and universally valid. From a traditional Left perspective, ID politics is the answer to fascism. It crashes patriotism and the bond with the soil, in favour of newly-formed global leagues.

The Left's enthusiasm for ID politics can also be explained in purely political terms: the Left is committed to the oppressed and the expansion of oppressed discourses (Blacks, women, Jews, gays and so on) provided a major opportunity for the left to broaden its popular support.

ID politics promised to break the rigid class system. It promised to dismantle the hegemony of aristocracy as well the dominance of mammon and socioeconomic status. When one identifies primarily as a gay, a Black, a Jew, a woman or a feminist, it doesn't really matter whether one is rich, an aristocrat or penniless. Within the context of ID politics, education is not a divisive factor either. Biology is often the primary criterion. Marginal identification and ID politics offer an attainable image of 'inclusive' equality that can compete with and even defeat fascist populism. Once united by the 'primacy of the symptom', social status and 'capital' become less important.

A fundamental question remains. What does this new form of social grouping and political bonding have to do with opposition to capital accumulation or the dominance of the power of mammon and mammonism? The answer is nothing.

In retrospect, the Left's decision to embrace ID politics

sealed its fate as an effective force for social change. It helped the Left to accept its detachment from struggling classes, their values and interests. It marked a clear separation between the Left and socialism and even Left and the people. In the most peculiar way, it prepared the ground for the surge in popularity of New Right, Donald Trump in the USA, UKIP in Britain, the National Front in France and so on.

Divide and Conquer

Like the Left, Jewish intelligentsia found ID politics a powerful and helpful tool. Diaspora Jews are often intimidated by nationalism, rootedness, patriotism, fascism and popular movements in general. From a Jewish political perspective, ID politics is a pragmatic tool to weaken national cohesiveness: it breaks the so-called 'White' and the Christian into sub-groups. ID politics enables the Jews to tackle the anti-Semitism that in the eyes of some Jews is 'prevalent' within a host nation. From a Jewish political perspective, a society divided into marginal segments by ethnicity, gender, sexual orientation as well as opposing interest groups, is much safer than a unified nation united behind a strong leader.

The traditional Left's opposition to aristocracy and elitism can be grasped in economic, ideological and political terms but the Jewish battle with the aristocracy is more complicated. The Jewish elite sees traditional aristocracy as an imminent threat as well as potential competitors. Jews are often intimidated by 'unwelcoming' dominant groups. The attitude of traditional English aristocracy towards Jews can be fairly described as rather cold[16]. The American WASP elite's reaction to Jews was no different. American Jews can't forget nor forgive the exclusive American country clubs that prevented their entry. ID politics serves to break the hostile elite. It dismantles the danger imposed by the 'anti-Semitic goy' by dividing the alleged 'enemy' and its leadership into new and different godless tribes.

ID politics may provide a new form of cohesion for the Left and the West, but for the people of the book, ID politics is as old as the Jews. Like ID politics, Jewish tribalism is biologically[17]-driven and ethno-centric by nature, and it also works on a global socio-political level. Like ID politics, Jewish tribal ideology defies geography, borders and rootedness.

Like ID politics, Jewish tribalism conveys an inclusive and welcoming image. It promises the club members equal opportunity to celebrate his or her privileges, yet club membership is exclusive and defined by strict ethno-centrism that is blood-related (being born to a Jewish mother). The club may open its gates occasionally to converts; however, adopting the Jewish religion is in itself a long tedious process and not a welcoming one.

---

16. An interesting glimpse into British aristocracy's animosity towards Jewish bankers is depicted in the 1934 Alfred L. Werker film House of Rothschild. The film chronicles the rise of the Rothschild family. It delves into the European aristocracy and its anti-Jewish sentiments towards the Rothschild family and its banking network.

17. Though Jews do not form a racial continuum, Judaism, Jewish culture and politics are always racially oriented.

Dividing society into ID sectarian groups can be understood as an attempt to break nations and people into a manifold of godless communities that are interconnected globally. If I am correct here, then one way to evaluate the ID apparatus is as a successful attempt to 'Jewify' the social order on a global scale. If Zionism is realized as a modest, however non-ethical, promise for a land, ID politics aims at a global transformation – it pushes for a planet divided by Identitarian tribalism. We are dealing with the emergence of a powerful new form of exceptionalism that emulates Jewish tribalism on a global scale.

Like political correctness, ID politics, although ostensibly driven by 'identification', destroys authenticity. ID politics eliminates the possibility of authentic self and replaces it with a delusional biologically-oriented group politics that is determined by the primacy of a symptom (skin colour, sexual orientation, ethnicity etc.). What attracts Americans such as homosexual Julie to identify politically as a gay, or Moishe, a Jew to identify as a Zionist, or Kelvin to identify as black? After all, Julie, Moishe and Kelvin are part of larger national collectives. We have to grasp the mechanism that drives some Western subjects away from the larger national ethos into marginal, exclusive and segregated biologically-oriented ghettos.

Homonationalism vs The Queer International

In her 2012 book *Israel/Palestine and the Queer International*,

Sarah Schulman examines this question. Unable to separate herself from her cultural Jewish upbringing, Schulman's political universe is replete with different binary oppositions; Jew/Goy, Israeli/Palestinian, man/woman, gay/heterosexual and so on. Apparently the binary opposition between 'homonationalism' and 'The Queer International' was so disturbing to Schulman that she devoted a book to the topic.

Schulman defines homonationalism as a contemporary phenomenon most prevalent in some liberal Western countries where "white gays, lesbians and bisexuals won a full range of rights ... they become accepted and realigned with patriotic or nationalistic ideologies of their countries."[18]

The notion of homonationalism is particularly relevant to Israel, since the Jewish state has been very successful in mobilizing its patriotic gay community. It has managed to recruit the vast majority of its gay population to advertise the perception that Israel is way ahead of its neighbours as far as gay rights are concerned.

As an American "progressive Jew" and committed to the notion of *"Tikkun Olam,"*[19] Schulman is disturbed by homonationalism in general and Israeli homonationalism in particular. She would prefer gays and lesbians to be primarily committed to a cosmopolitan political discourse defined by their sexual orientation. This is where her notion of the Queer International comes into play. Schulman is aiming for a "worldwide movement that brings queer liberation and

18. Sarah Schulman: Israel/Palestine and the Queer International, pg 104
19. Tikun Olam - the (unfounded) belief that the Jews posses knowledge of how to make the world a better place.

feminism to the principle of international autonomy from occupation, colonialism, and globalized capital." She advocates for the cosmopolitanisation of the symptom, in practice, the Bolshevisation of the libidinal.

And yet, Schulmann leaves the fundamental question unanswered: why do so many gays in Israel prefer to identify with their national and patriotic surroundings rather than with a cosmopolitan, sexually-oriented ideology? Apparently most people, including gays, lesbians and transsexuals, accept a clear dichotomy between their sexual orientation and their political identification. It also seems natural that a country's LGBTQ citizens would be thankful to a society or culture that liberates them and respects their needs and rights.

Since the vast majority of healthy people spend most of their time out of bed, it makes sense that sexual orientation is not the primary focus of civil and political life. For most people, including the LGBTQ community, health, education and work are more crucial. Furthermore, Schulman's so-called progressive expectation of homosexuals, that they be devoted primarily to ID politics and 'Queer Universal' issues is abusive: it imposes on the individual an ideological collectivism and epistemological mantra based solely on that individual's sexual orientation.

Interventionism

As an enthusiastic Jewish pro-Palestinian advocate and mouthpiece for 'Queer International', Schulman is up against

Palestinian gay academic Joseph Massad. According to him, the heterosexual/homosexual binary opposition is foreign to the Orient – it is basically "a Western apparatus imposing concepts of homosexuality on sex between men."[20] For Massad, gays and lesbians are not universal categories, and the attempt to universalize them is the direct outcome of human rights activists who project their own symptom at the expense of their 'solidarity subject.'

His argument is coherent and deserves attention. Like Heidegger, and other developed minds (people who accept that rootedness shapes our outlook), Massad considers the human subject to be a product of his/her culture, language, rituals, geography and so on. Schulman's approach is the outcome of a naive phenomenological anthropocentric school of thought. Like many other progressives and ID activists of her generation, she believes that people are the 'authors of their own biographies', and that these biographies are somehow universal and exchangeable.

This ideological clash is crucial. Massad proposes that the universalization of the symptom, as suggested by Schulman, and the Queer International is just another form of Western immoral interventionism. It imposes and projects Western liberal categories on others.

LGBT and feminists´ rights activists have been utilized to promote neocon and Zionist conflicts. It is known that, in advance of the so-called 'War on Terror' and the Anglo-American invasion of Afghanistan, women's rights groups

20. Ibid pg 66

60

helped produce the moral groundwork for the conflict. The West's opposition to Putin and Russian politics is supported and sometimes waged by gay campaigns and 'pussy rioters.'[21] And gay rights groups have, however unconsciously, prepared the ground for a possible military intervention in central Africa[22]. Is it a coincidence that ID political and progressive campaigns often precede neocon imperialist wars?

On Blindness

The Schulman/Massad dispute is a fascinating illustration of the intellectual black hole at the heart of the ID political discourse. Like the old Left's failure to bond with the working class, ID political advocate Schulman expresses frustration with homonationalism. For some reason, these Israeli homosexuals are subscribing to the 'Zionist' call instead of joining the cosmopolitan (pseudo-Bolshevist) queer revolution.

It seems as if both the Old Left and the New Left, are frustrated by the apathy of their solidarity subjects. Neither the worker nor the marginal subject, in this case, the

---

21. Pussy Riot - a Russian feminist musical protest group based in Moscow. According to some Internet sources they are supported by the National Endowment for Democracy.

22. It has been argued that African leaders' populist opposition to gay rights (Robert Mugabe, Yahya Jammeh and Yoweri Museveni) is motivated by clear defiance of Western intervention. At the same time, the current Western campaign for LGBT Rights in Africa can be realised as a pretext for just another 'moral' interventionist conflict.

homosexual, properly heeds the 'progressive' political call. Just as the worker defies or simply ignores the notion of the revolution, the Israeli homosexual, so it seems, prefers to join the Israeli hasbara campaign rather than letting his sexual orientation guide all of his political decisions.

I can think of two possible explanations for this failure at the heart of New Left, Liberal and progressive thinking. It may be that both the old and the new Left have repeatedly failed to identify the symptom; instead they invent or impose a symptom as Massad suggests. But people are more than just a set of symptoms.

In other words, 'Being' is more complicated than a mere dialectical-materialist formula: socio-economic status, skin colour or sexual orientation. As such, 'Being' is within the domain of the inexpressible. Being is within the domain of the 'Lacanian Real,' for it is unattainable. The attempt to reduce it into a set of binaries is an inhumane, futile project that is moving us all towards disaster.

Victimhood vs Whiteness

In comparison with the general failure of the good old union-based Left, New Left and ID politics have enjoyed outstanding success. At least in the West, liberals, New Left and Identitarian merchants have managed to locate themselves at the centre of mainstream political discourse, culture and media attention. At least for the time being, they dominate the mainstream media.

Meanwhile, American blue-collar workers have been

targeted for constant humiliation. They have been sneered at as White people, White nationalists, occasionally White supremacists, and often enough, as rednecks. When a black person doesn't follow the ID political protocol like British Momentum leader Jackie Walker[23] or the French comedian star Dieudonné M'bala M'bala, she or he is immediately excised from the list of multicultural heroes and is relocated into the 'racist bigots' box. This happened to Black Lives Matter. Once they expressed their solidarity with other oppressed people (Palestinians) they were very quickly taught what matters for real.

We have to grasp why people would voluntarily adopt exclusive segregation over large and inclusive unity. What is it that pushes Julie, Moishe and Kelvin whom we met earlier on, to adopt sectarian and exclusive politics?

ID politics is sustained by the perception of victimhood. Like the Jew who is threatened by an imaginary White, Christian, Goy, within the ID political cosmos, the woman is, as if by a law of physics, oppressed by the male, the Black is threatened by the redneck, and the Muslim is chased by the Islamophobe. To use Hillary Clinton's 'progressive' terminology, it is a political world view that is defined by the 'deplorables.'

We are dealing here with identities that are defined by a sense of victimhood and a clear notion of an oppressor. ID politics sets a transparent binary opposition between the

---

23 Momentum vice-chair and British Labour activist Jackie Walker was heckled at a Labour party anti-Semitism conference, after she criticised Holocaust Memorial Day for not including non-Jewish genocide victims. Following the event Walker was suspended from the Labour Party.

disadvantaged and the privileged. Black and White, woman and man, gay and heterosexual, Muslim and the West.

But what about the Jew and the Goy? It would be somehow wrong to locate the Jews amongst the 'disadvantaged' while throwing the 'Goy' into the 'privileged' basket. After all, Jews are amongst the richest and most educated ethnic groups in the West. Their elite is vastly overrepresented in Western finance, politics, media and culture. They are clearly privileged.

Furthermore, what is a Goy? A brief attempt to figure that out would reveal that the Goy is basically the rest of humanity or simply, humanity. Accordingly, Jewish ID politics creates a binary opposition juxtaposing the Jew and humanity. This seems a perpetual problem for the Jew and explains the historic role of Jewish ID politics in evoking anti-Jewish sentiments.

'Whiteness' as a concept counteracts this difficulty at the core of Jewish ID politics. Whiteness breaks the imaginary 'Goy' (gentile) category into a set of marginal groups. Instead of Jew vs humanity as a binary opposition, we are now dealing with Jew vs White, Jew vs anti-Semite, Jew vs Jihadi terrorist and so on. On each of these 'battlegrounds' the Jewish Identitarian activist seeks different allies.

When it comes to Jew vs White, the progressive Jew sides with the Civil Rights movement and Black Lives Matter. But Jewish Identitarians form alliances with all sorts of oppressed groups. They will join women in their fight against the White male. They will fight with the immigrants against the White nationalist. They will fight with the Muslims against White islamophobia.[24] Yet there is a looming problem. The opposition is missing. Despite the many battles for a better world, hardly anyone out there really self-identifies as a White male, White Islamophobe, White nationalist or White supremacist.

For different reasons that may have to do with a certain element of privilege, people who happen to be white hardly notice the colour of their own skin. Whiteness is an identity category that at least momentarily, is imposed on white people and is foreign to most of them. It is worth mentioning that the few who proactively identify politically as White, are often those who campaign for White rights. In other words, they claim to be discriminated against. They insist, for instance, that if diversity is the way forward white people shouldn't be excluded.

Seemingly, the call against Whiteness is a negative dialectic permutation of biological determinism. If anti-Semitism is defined as 'hating Jews for being Jews', then ID political misanthropy is a similar form of biologically-oriented hatred. It hates the White for being white. It hates men for being men ('all men are rapists') and so on. We are dealing with a political ideology that is guided by projection. The anti-White Identitarians, for instance, attribute their own sectarian ideology to people who happen to be born white.

Jewishness, as I discuss in my book *The Wandering Who*,

---

24. Some Jews will also join forces with ultra-Right wing groups such as English Defense League (EDL) supporting their battle against 'Jihadi terror' and the transformation of London into what the hardcore Zionist journalist Melanie Philips calls "Londonistan."

can be defined as different forms of celebrating chosenness, clearly a form of privilege. Among these, Zionism is the most assertive, belligerent and successful contemporary Jewish political precept. But if we want to grasp the success of Zionism, if we want to understand why Schulman perceives that Israeli gays favour homonationalism, we have to understand that Zionism, at least traditionally, is a radical form of empowerment and not a part of the New Left ID political affinity for victimhood.

In order to examine Zionist ideological thought let's look into the contempt expressed by early Zionists toward their fellow Jews.

This is how A.D. Gordon,[25] the founder of Labour Zionism expressed his: "We are a parasitic people. We have no roots in the soil, there is no ground beneath our feet. And we are parasites not only in an economic sense, but in spirit, in thought, in poetry, in literature, and in our virtues, our ideals, our higher human aspirations."

The Zionist Marxist youth magazine, *Hashomer Hatzair*, stated in 1936: "The Jew is a caricature of a normal, natural human being, both physically and spiritually. As an individual in society he revolts and throws off the harness of social obligations, knows no order nor discipline."[26]

Ber Borochov, the Jewish socialist revolutionary also didn't approve of the Jew: "The enterprising spirit of the Jew is

25. D Gordon, 1856–1922, was an early Zionist ideologue.

26. Shomer 'Weltanschauung', Hashomer Hatzair, December 1936, p 26. As cited by Lenni Brenner http://www.marxists.de/middleast/brenner/cho2.htm#n10

irrepressible. He refuses to remain a proletarian. He will grab at the first opportunity to advance to a higher rung in the social ladder."[27]

Early Zionist thinkers were apparently galvanized by a deep revulsion for the diaspora Jews. They resisted the primacy of the Jewish symptom. They preached for a radical metamorphosis of the Jew. They promised that Zionism would civilize the diaspora Jew by means of a manufactured homecoming.

Zionism was, at least in its early stages, totally opposed to a discourse of victimhood. It was a unique chapter in Jewish history, when Jews looked in the mirror and were brave enough to admit, at least to themselves, that they were repulsed by what they saw. They vowed to change, striving to become a 'people like all other people.'

Examining early Zionism in terms of the relationships between the political and the human explains the Zionist appeal. Like the fascism that followed three decades later, Zionism synthesized utopia and nostalgia, being/becoming, the dream and the Real, the Left and the Right. It was repelled by the present, it insisted upon change. But the future it promised was nostalgic in nature. It was rooted in an imaginary past of phantasmic origins (the biblical narrative). One hundred and twenty years before Donald Trump and forty years before Hitler, early Zionists promised the Jews that they could 'once again' be a great people.

---

27. The Economic Development of the Jewish People, Ber Borochov, 1916
http://www.angelfire.com/il2/borochov/eco.html

Ultimately, Zionism was a colossal failure in its attempt to change the Jew. The symptoms that disturbed Herzl, Nordau, Borochov, A. D. Gordon, Ben Former and others, are more prominent than ever. Israel is everything but a proletarian society and its appalling ethical record is noted by numerous critical UN reports on human rights and crimes against humanity. Yet, Zionism was a political success. In less than six decades, it fulfilled its promise to the Jews. It stole Palestine and, with vast international support, made it into a Jewish national homeland at the expense of its indigenous population. Pro-Israel Jewish lobbies dominate Western politics by various means, and the existence of the Jews-only state has yet to be seriously challenged.

Unlike early Zionism which was distinguished by some intensive self-criticism, ID politics is an exercise in uncritical self-love: in early Zionism, the overtly assertive and militant ID movement was characterised by Jews taking responsibility for their actions as well as their fate. But contemporary ID politics advocates the complete absence of personal responsibility.

Within the context of New Left ID politics, it is always someone else who is at fault. The feminist blames the male chauvinist, the Black blames the racist White, the Palestinian blames the Zionists. And even within the realm of post-and-contemporary Zionist discourse, the Jews blame anti-Semites and send their children to tour Auschwitz, the Mecca of Jewish suffering.

Early Zionism promised liberation by means of empowerment, but New Left and ID politics package false emancipation with victimhood.

Contemporary ID politics substitutes responsibility with collective paralysis. This is an intractable flaw: one cannot be emancipated if one's condition is someone else's fault. Early Zionism was appealing because the ideology led to a self-administrated (imaginary) metamorphosis. ID politics preaches stagnation by means of victimhood – by setting binaries between the disadvantaged (the innocent oppressed) and the privileged (the oppressor). By deflecting responsibility, it requires no self-reflection, and neither seeks nor offers liberation or change.

Early Zionism prevailed because it was fuelled by self-loathing and a longing for a nationalist redemption. But that phase of honesty was a rare moment in Jewish history. Zionism quickly morphed into a tidal wave of self-love suffocated with hubris that matured into blindness. While early Zionists tended to agree with the 'anti-Semite', pointing out the Jewish symptoms that brought disaster to the Jews, the contemporary Zionist paints the 'anti-Semite' label broadly and includes those who draw attention to Jewish political and cultural deficiencies. Within the context of Jewish contemporary ID politics, the Jew, like the Black, the woman and the gay, is reduced to a victim.

Some Jews and particularly Israelis are confused by the shift from early Zionism to 'post-Zionism.' Contemporary Zionism is in a split-minded state in which the Jew is both oppressor and victim. Some Israeli academics and intellectuals, such as Uri Avnery, decry the Jewish wail of anti-Semitism as an attempt to avoid both political responsibility and an understanding of consequences of Israeli and Jewish actions.

Considering the significant role of the Jewish progressive intelligentsia in the formation of ID political thought globally, we are left with a crucial question: why does Zionist ID politics aim for empowerment yet, Left ID politics settle for victimhood?

Welcome to Dystopia

"Melancholy and Utopia are heads and tails of the same coin" – **Günter Grass**

ISIS, Scotland, Brexit, Trump - The Politics of Mimicry

What connects the following phenomena?

Nearly half the Scots voted to split from Britain.

More than half the Brits chose to quit the EU.

Donald Trump became an American president and hundreds of European Muslims are fighting with Jihadi militant groups in Syria.

These developments are indeed intrinsically linked yet in the intellectual desert in which we live, few have attempted to understand the connection. We are at a point where the boundaries of our curiosity are limited by correctness and sectarian sensitivities.

From a political perspective, the call for Scottish independence, the victory of the UK's 'Leave' campaign (Brexit) and Trump's victory are all rather obviously direct outcomes of a growing shift in the West towards patriotism, nationalism, rootedness and tribalism. But also, young European Muslims journey to Syria in response to the same basic desire. From both a philosophical and dialectical perspective, 'Jihadi' identification and European or American nationalism are the antithesis of the sectarian ID politics that provides only a lame, inauthentic mimicry.

As we discussed in previous chapters, the West has undergone decades of relentless, divisive attacks on patriotic and family values and national identity. The flag, the church, the traditional family, and basically anything that resembles or is attached to rootedness – all have come under attack. This offensive has been led primarily on ideological and intellectual fronts by those who subscribe to progressive, liberal and New Left ideas. This may even include Left icons such as Noam Chomsky who, for years, have been calling for the abolition of borders and states (except, of course, for the Jewish State).

The New Left has advocated that traditional, national, patriotic discourse be replaced with identity politics which, as we explored earlier, pretends to promote authentic thinking but actually replaces authenticity with 'identification.' The response to this general promotion of identity politics and its attendant rules of political correctness has been a renewed interest in tribal, patriotic and nationalist ideas.

In order to grasp the emerging nationalist counter-culture we will examine the historic evolution within Zionism from the perspective of ID politics. If you wonder why I look at Zionism, the answer is embarrassingly simple. Zionist ideologists were, I believe, ahead of anyone else in identifying the threat inherent in ID politics.[28]

In the 1970s, identity politics became popular within the

_____

28. As we will see later, even in the USA, it was the ultra-Zionist Breitbart.com that emerged as the most popular as well as populist opposition to ID politics.

Jewish Left and amongst progressives. Americans and Brits who attend socialist and solidarity gatherings are familiar with those who launch their comments with, "as a Jew I believe..." or "as a Jew I demand..." But it was the Zionists and Israeli nationalist ideologists who were the first to realize that the 'as a' culture – the cult that pushes people to identify as sectarian collectives (as a Jew, as a Black, as a Muslim) – might be effective in dividing the gentiles, but it wasn't "good for the Jews."

Zionist institutions were quick to capitalize on the authenticity gulf that had been created by identity politics. The Zionist mantra to the diaspora Jew was: "Instead of identifying 'as a' Jew in New York, Paris or London, come to Israel and ... *be* a Jew." In other words, come to Israel, join the IDF, learn to drive a tank or fly an F-16, spend your weekends on a Tel Aviv beach, unite with your people, *be* a Jew amongst Jews.

This call appealed to many young diaspora Jews. The IDF is saturated with lone soldiers who landed in their considered promised land to fill their Jewish identity with practical and spiritual meaning.

ISIS offers the same to young Western Muslims. Instead of identifying 'as a Muslim' within a hostile society that is godless, materialist and bans the burkini, the Islamic State and other Jihadi organisations offer their followers the opportunity, instead of living 'as Muslims,' to come to 'the Islamic State' and ... *be* Muslims.[29] The Zionist and ISIS appeal

---

29. The above is by no means an endorsement of Isis' version of Islam.

are basically identical reactions to New Left ID politics.

But the rise of nationalism is everywhere. Almost half of the Scots preferred to split from the U.K. Instead of subscribing to watery multicultural Britain or identifying 'as Scottish,' which hardly means anything – they chose instead, *being* Scottish.

It would be impossible to refer to those events without looking at the recent Brexit referendum, where the majority of Brits voted to leave the EU, believing that such a move could reinstate their patriotic union. Apparently, most Brits want to *be* British for real, rather than subscribing to a score of vague European identities, identities that they largely fail to grasp.

The popularity of Trump and Sanders amongst both Republican and Democratic voters was also driven by opposition to the Identitarian 'as a' culture. Both Trump and Sanders offered unifying collective views that favoured nationalism and rootedness as opposed to sectarianism and Identitarian world views.

The question is, why were the Zionists and subsequent Israelis amongst the first to diagnose the dangers inherent in identity politics? Why did their institutions reject the New Left mantra? Why were the Israelis the first to oppose the progressive 'as a' (Jew) manner of speech?

I can think of a few answers. In comparison to Jews in matters of ID politics, most Western cultures are relative neophytes. Judaism and Jewish culture have been engaged in identity culture, i.e., implementing strategies and defence mechanisms to preserve a 'Jewish tribal cohesiveness' for the last 2000 years. For instance, the Jewish *Kosher* diet kept the Jew from eating with the Goy and thus sustained segregation and exclusivity.   Such cultural elements encourage a sense of togetherness, collective loyalty, unity and (amongst the Jews) a shared fate.

On a deeper level, if ID politics and cultural Marxism are largely Jewish political schools of thought, it is no surprise that the opposition to cultural Marxism and ID politics are also largely put forth by Jews. In other words, if cultural Marxism or ID politics are Jewish revolutionary 'diseases,' Jews were the most able and first to resist these symptoms simply because they possess the intellectual, cultural and spiritual anti-bodies.   It is even reasonable to posit that Jewish revolutionaries found the answer to ID politics even before identity politics was born.

In 1936, thousands of revolutionary Jews travelled to Spain to fight the army of General Francisco Franco, whom they believed to be a fascist.[30] The young revolutionaries were motivated by a 'proletarian' cosmopolitan ideology of global liberation. They marched heroically to Spain, willing to give their lives in the name of the international working class. But when they landed in Catalonia they discovered

---

30. It is important to mention that a growing number of contemporary historians accept that General Franco wasn't a 'Fascist', in the most conventional meaning of Fascism. Franco wasn't a 'National Socialist.' He was a Catholic patriot. However, Franco was indeed supported by Fascist Germany and Italy (while the Republican government was supported by Stalin's USSR).

that one quarter of the Spanish International Brigade were Jewish and the lingua franca was Yiddish. Apparently, the real workers didn't make it to Spain. They had to stay home and get up in the morning to go to work.

There is a devastating insight attached to this story. While young Jewish warriors travelled to Spain in an attempt to be real 'workers', real workers, who had no need to attempt anything, stayed at home. Unlike the heroic young Jews, these folks knew they were workers.

This is the best explanation I can offer for the systematic failure of the Left; globally, historically and philosophically. For the real proletariat, home, labour and productivity are not theoretical constructs. As opposed to the imaginary state of the 'ought to be' or the social Utopia, they are actually existentially rooted in 'Being.'

As such, true proletarian existence belongs within the domain of Right thinking and this may explain why blue-collar workers in the UK and the USA vote UKIP and Trump. Bonding with the Left may, for these workers, simply contradict their proletarian essentiality.

The Red Jews who travelled to Spain ended up fighting in Jewish legions because ID politics and Left-orientation are largely a Jewish intellectual domain that is actually quite foreign to working people. Those Jews were engaged in an early form of ID politics (with the working class), yet the more they invested in their identifications, the more Yiddish-speaking was their brigade.

Comparing contemporary young Westerners who join ISIS to the 1936 'Red' Jewish Spanish saga is revealing. The ISIS enthusiast travels to Syria because he or she wants to 'be' a Muslim rather than just identifying 'as a' Muslim. The young New York Jew joins the IDF because he or she wants to 'be' a Jew. The Scots want to 'be' Scots and the Brits want to 'be' Brits. But the Jewish revolutionary travelled to Barcelona in order to stop being a Jew and become, once and for all, 'a proletarian.'

These Jews engaged in an illusory identification exercise. By the time they made it to the battlefront, surrounded by other revolutionary Jews and receiving their orders in Yiddish, they were more segregated than their ancestors in the ghetto. The revolutionary Jews didn't believe in God or keep the Sabbath but they were killing Spanish Catholics and often burning their churches, something Rabbinical Jews never did. The 1936 naive Jewish revolutionary attempt to identify 'as a' cosmopolitan proletariat backfired; those young combatants ended up in the Jewish military ghetto fighting real and rooted Spanish patriots.[31]

Jewish liberal identity politics may be inconsistent and incoherent; progressive Jews tend to oppose racism, yet operate within Jewish-only groups that are racially-orientated. Yet, Zionism seems more consistent. It is a racial movement but, unlike its progressive counterpart, is totally open about it.

A few days before the 2016 American presidential election, we learned from the Israeli press that, at least in

---

31. I have lost my last Jewish peace loving friend over this expose of the delusional intent at the core of the Spanish International Brigade. The topic is still a sacred taboo within Left circles.

Israel, Donald Trump won the popular vote. While in the US 70% of American Jews voted for Hillary Clinton and her liberal agenda, in Israel more than 50% of American expatriates chose Trump. This result is consistent with the Zionist defiance of ID politics. Zionism provides an (illusory) sense of 'rootedness' and 'belonging.' The Israeli attitude towards migrant communities is brutal. Israel is not committed to liberal values. In Israel, Palestinians are discriminated against.

Whether we approve the Zionist message or not, it is hard to deny that Trump's Israeli voters, who must believe that if a separation wall is good for Israel it may also be good for America, are at least consistent. They are Jews and they think like Jews. They accept that if exceptionalism works for Israel, it may well work for America. Later in the book we will find out that the Alt-Right movement, which supported Donald Trump and was integrated into his team once he was elected, was in fact infested with Zionist agitators and pro-Israel Lobbyists. The Israeli-American expatriates seem to conclude that what is good for Israel is good for America and vice versa. It is hard to deny that this worldview is almost as consistent as it is unethical.

History and Repression

History is commonly considered as the attempt to produce a structured account of the past. It claims to tell us what really happened but it generally fails to do so. What history does instead is to provide a narrative of the past that conceals our shame and hides the various events, incidents and occurrences in our past with which we cannot cope. As practiced, history can be regarded as a system of suppression. This places the real historian in a role similar to that of the psychoanalyst: both aim to reveal the repressed. For the psychoanalyst, it is the unconscious mind, for the historian, it is our collective shame.

How many historians really engage in such a task? How many historians are courageous enough to open Pandora's Box? How many historians are brave enough to challenge slavery for real? How many historians, for instance, dare to ask why, time after time, Jews suffer? Can Palestinian historians explain how is it that after more than a century of struggle, their current capital (Ramallah) has become a NGO haven largely funded by light Zionists such as George Soros and his Open Society Institute? Can the Brits explain to themselves why, in their own Imperial War Museum, they erected a permanent Holocaust exhibition dedicated to the destruction of one people only, namely the Jews? Shouldn't the Brits be more courageous and look into some of the many disasters they themselves have inflicted on others? And if the Brits are genuinely troubled by the Holocaust, maybe they should dedicate a corner of that exhibit to how and why the Empire closed its gates to Jewish refugees from Europe in the late 1930s.

Shouldn't the Americans do the same? Clearly, they have an impressive back catalogue of disasters from which to choose. But like the Brits, the Americans prefer to erect Holocaust museums rather than examine their own shame.

The *Guardian* vs Athens

The past is dangerous territory; it contains some inconvenient stories. No wonder a sincere investigative historian is often perceived as a public enemy. However, the New Left has invented an academic method to tackle the issue. The 'progressive' historian functions to produce a 'politically correct', 'inoffensive' tale of the past. This narrative zigzags its way, paying its dues to the concealed and produces endless *ad hoc* deviations that leave the 'repressed' untouched. The progressive historical account is there to produce a non-essentialist, safe account of the past. A paradigm of this approach is often provided by the *Guardian* newspaper.

For instance, the *Guardian* bans any criticism of Jewish culture or Jewishness, yet it provides a televised platform for two rabid Zionists to discuss Arab culture and 'Islamism.'[32] The media outlet does not mind offending 'Islamists' or British 'nationalists' but is very careful not to hurt any LGBT or Jewish sensitivities.

Such versions of culture or history are impervious to truthfulness, coherence, consistency or integrity. In fact, the progressive exchange is the antithesis of the guardian of the truth; it is actually 'the guardian of the discourse' and I am referring here to New Left and liberal discourses in particular.

---

32. I am referring here to a Guardian-televised discussion between Israeli ultra-ethnic cleansing enthusiast historian Benny Morris and the newspaper's own Jonathan Freedland. http://www.guardian.co.uk/world/video/2009/sep/08/benny-morris-jonathan-freedland

But surely there is an alternative to the 'progressive' attitude to the past. The 'real historian'[33] is actually a philosopher, an essentialist, a thinker who posits the question: "What does it mean to be in the world within the context of temporality and Being?" This true inquisitor attempts to answer the question of what does it take to 'live amongst others?' He or she transcends the singular, the particular and the personal, searching for that which truly drives our past, present and future, namely the essence. The real historian dwells on 'being and time' and is searching for a humanist lesson and an ethical insight while looking into the poetry, the art, the beauty, the search for logos, i.e., reason. The real toiler has to dig into the fear, dredging out the concealed, for he or she knows that, within the repressed, is the kernel of the truth.

Leo Strauss provides a useful insight in that regard. In his writings, the late German-American political philosopher contends that Western civilization oscillates between two intellectual and spiritual poles – Athens and Jerusalem. Athens, as we explored before, is the birthplace of reason, philosophy, art, science and the logos. Jerusalem, on the other hand, is the city of God where God's law prevails. The philosopher, the true historian, or the essentialist, for that matter, is the Athenian, 'the guardian of the truth.' The Jerusalemite is 'the guardian of the discourse', the one who keeps the gate, in order to maintain law and

---

33. If history is the attempt to narrate the past as we move along, the 'Real Historian' is the scholar who attempts to shape, re-shape, visit, re-visit or in short revise the past.

order at the expense of ecstasies, poetry, beauty, reason and truth.

Spielberg vs Tarantino

Hollywood provides us with an example of the oscillation between Athens and Jerusalem: between the Jerusalemite guardian and the essentialist, public enemy Athenian. On the Left side of the map we find Steven Spielberg, the progressive genius, the master of correctness. On his Right we meet *poesis* itself, Quentin Tarantino, the essentialist rebel.

Spielberg produces the ultimate, sanitized historical epic. The story is based on facts cherry-picked to produce a premeditated, pseudo-ethical tale that maintains the righteous discourse, law and order and, most importantly, the primacy of Jewish suffering: *Schindler's List* (1993) and *Munich* (2005). Spielberg brings to life a grand retrospective epic. His tactic is usually pretty simple. He juxtaposes a vivid, transparent, binary opposition: Nazis vs Jews, Israeli vs Palestinian, North vs South, Righteousness vs Slavery. In short, it is 'progressive' vs 'reactionary.' Somehow, we always know in advance with whom he sides, we know who the baddies are.

Binary opposition is a safe route. It provides a clear distinction between the *Kosher* and the 'forbidden.' But Spielberg is not a banal producer. He allows a highly calculated and carefully meditated oscillation. In a pseudo-empathic gesture, he will allow a single Nazi into the family of the gentle. A Palestinian may be a victim. Small variations are allowed so long as the main frame of the discourse remains intact. Spielberg is an expert guardian of discourse – and as a master of his art-form, he can easily maintain his audience's attention for a three-hour long entertaining cinematic cocktail of pseudo-historic/factual mishmash. All you need to do is eat your popcorn and follow the plot. By the movie's end, the pre-digested ethical message is safely replanted at the centre of your self-loving universe.

Unlike Spielberg, Tarantino is not committed to any appearance of factual narrative; he may even repel historicity. Tarantino treats 'the message' or morality as inconsequential. Tarantino is a reactionary essentialist, he is interested in human nature, in 'Being', and he seems to be fascinated in particular with vengeance and its universality. His totally far-fetched 2009 movie, *Inglorious Basterds*, portrays Jewish and Israeli Goy-hatred better than any academic study could ever do.

His fictional cinematic creation of a vengeful, murderous WWII Jewish commando unit throws light on the devastating contemporary reality of the Jewish lobbies' relentless push for more and more global conflicts against Iran, Syria, Libya and beyond. But *Inglorious Basterds* may have a universal appeal as well: in the aftermath of 9/11, the Old Testament's eye-for-an-eye has become the driving force in Anglo-American politics.

Abe'le vs Django

This spiritual clash between Jerusalemite Spielberg and Athenian Tarantino is further illustrated in their portrayals of slaves and slavery.

The history of slavery in America is problematic and, for obvious reasons, many aspects of this history still lay deeply buried. Spielberg and Tarantino share little ground in their cinematic accounts of slavery and its effects.

In his 2012 historical epic, *Lincoln*, Spielberg turns Abraham Lincoln into a genuine 'moral interventionist' who, against all political odds, abolished slavery. I suspect Spielberg knows enough American history to gather that his cinematic account is a crude attempt at concealment. He must know that the humanitarian aspect of the anti-slavery political campaign was a mere pretext for a bloody war driven by economic objectives. But, while peppering his tale with a few historical anecdotes, he does his bit to keep the shame shoved deep under the carpet. His Lincoln is cherished as a morally-driven hero of human brotherhood and the entire plot shows all the symptoms of a contemporary AIPAC lobby assault on the Capitol. As one of the arch guardians of the discourse, Spielberg has successfully fulfilled his task. He has added a substantial cinematic layer to ensure that America's true shame remains undisturbed.

Of course, Spielberg's take on Lincoln was applauded by the Jewish press. In the Tablet magazine, they called President Avraham (Abraham) Lincoln Avinu (our father,

Hebrew)[34]. According to the publication, 'Avraham,' is the definitive good Jew: "As imagined by Spielberg and Kushner, Lincoln's Lincoln is the ultimate mensch (merciful, Yiddish). He is a skilled natural psychologist, an interpreter of dreams, and a man blessed with an extraordinarily clever and subtle legal mind." In short, Spielberg transforms Abraham Lincoln into Abe'le who combines all the skills, the gifts and the traits of Moses (the leader), Freud (the wise) and Alan Dershowitz (the Zionist propaganda merchant). However, some Jews complained about the film. "As an American Jewish historian," writes Lance J. Sussman, "I'm afraid I have to say I am somewhat disappointed with the latest Spielberg film. So much of it is so good, but it would have been even better if he had put at least one Jew in the movie, somewhere."[35]

I guess that while Stephen Spielberg finds it hard to please the entire tribe. Quentin Tarantino doesn't even try as he's not trying to enshrine anyone. Through a phantasmic epic that never even purports to be history, *Django Unchained* (2012), digs out the darkest secrets of slavery. He scratches the concealed and, judging by the hostile reaction of another cinematic genius, Spike Lee, he clearly managed to get in pretty deep.

In a stylistic spectacle within the Western genre Tarantino dwells on every aspect we are advised to leave untouched. He deals with biological determinism, and White brutality.

34 http://www.tabletmag.com/jewish-arts-and-culture/116078/avraham-linoln-avinu

35 http://www.jewishjournal.com/oscars/article/spielbergs_lincoln_and_the_jews_an_untold_story

Then he turns his critical lens onto a segment of the slaves' passivity, subservience and collaboration.

The Athenian director builds a set of Greek mythological god-like characters; Django is the unruly king of revenge and Schultz, the German dentist turned bounty hunter, is the master of wit, kindness and humanity with a giant wisdom tooth shining over his caravan. Calvin Candie is the Hegelian (racist) Master and Stephen is the Hegelian Slave, emerging as the personification of social transformation. The relationship between Candie and Stephen is a profound yet subversive cinematic take on Hegel's master-slave dialectic.

In Hegel's dialectic, self-consciousness is constituted through a process of mirroring. In *Django Unchained*, Stephen the slave conveys the embodiment of subservience, but this is merely on the surface. In reality, Stephen is far more sophisticated and observant than his master Candie: he's on his way up. It is hard to determine whether Stephen is a collaborator or if he really runs the entire show. And yet in Tarantino's take, Hegel's dialectic is, somehow, compartmentalized. Django, once unchained, is impervious to the Hegelian dialectic spiel.

His incidental liberation induces in him a true spirit of revenge. He bends every rule including the 'rules of nature' (biological determinism) and, when given the opportunity, he kills the Master, the Slave and everyone else who happens to be around, By the time the epic is over, Django leaves Candie's plantation totally destroyed - a cinematic symbol of the dying antebellum American South and the

'Master Slave Dialectic.' Yet, as Django, together with his free wife Broomhilda von Shaft, rides his horse towards the rising sun, we are awakened to the far-fetched cinematic fantasy. In reality, in the world outside of the cinema where black lives really do not matter, Candie's plantation would most likely remain intact and Django would be chained up again. Tarantino cynically juxtaposes the dream (the cinematic reality) and reality (as we know it). By doing so he manages to illuminate the depth of misery entangled with the human condition and in particular on the Black reality in America.

Tarantino is no 'Guardian of the discourse.' Quite the opposite, he is the 'Daily Mail of truth,' the bitter enemy of stagnation. His work should be considered as an essentialist assault on political correctness and 'self-love.'

While America has been numbed by the exotic spell of correctness, Identitarian utopias and post-colonial studies, Tarantino and very few others have managed to sustain a spirit of Athenian resistance. Tarantino keeps turning over stones and unleashing vipers. Yet, as a devout Athenian he offers neither answers nor moral lessons. He leaves us perplexed yet ecstatic. For Tarantino the philosopher, dilemma is the existential essence. On the other hand, Spielberg, the Jerusalemite icon, provides answers. After all, within the 'progressive' politically-correct discourse, it is the answers, in retrospect, that determine what questions we are entitled to raise.

There is a shortage of Tarantinos and, if Leo Strauss is correct and Western civilisation can be seen as an oscillation between Athens and Jerusalem, then we desperately need many more Athenians and their reactionary essentialist reflections.

Thinking inside the Box

"Let us assume for the sake of argument that recent research had disproved once and for all every one of Marx's individual theses. Even if this were to be proved, every serious 'orthodox' Marxist would still be able to accept all such modern findings without reservation... Orthodox Marxism does not imply the uncritical acceptance of the results of Marx's investigations. It is not the 'belief' in this or that thesis, nor the exegesis of a 'sacred' book. On the contrary, orthodoxy refers exclusively to method." György Lukács, *History and Class Consciousness: Studies in Marxist Dialectics* (1923)

In his 1933 work, *The Mass Psychology of Fascism*, Jewish Marxist and Freudian psychoanalyst Wilhelm Reich attempted to explain the striking victory of 'reactionary' Fascism over 'progressive' Communism. Reich was desperate to rescue the relevance of revolutionary Marxism. In order to do so he formed a new 'post Marxist' theoretical outlook to explain why the Germans of his time favoured 'authoritarianism' over a 'preferable' communist revolution.

According to Reich, the attraction of reactionary and conservative politics and the inclination towards fascism is driven by a long history of rigid, authoritarian patriarchy which affects the family, parenting, primal education and eventually, society as a whole.

Of course, the remarkable popularity of fascism in Europe could have provided the scientifically-orientated Reich with a clear refutation of Marxist working class politics, theories and predictions. After all, dialectical Marxism had failed as a social theory as well as a methodical prophecy. But for some reason, he, like many other Jewish intellectuals of his time, decided to stick with Marx. Hoping to rescue what was left of dialectical materialism, and insisting that true communist political revolution would prevail once sexual repression was overthrown, Reich synthesized Marx and Freud into a 'Sex Revolution.'

Wilhelm Reich posited that sexual liberation on a mass scale would save Marxist dogmatism and working people as well. In chapter five of *The Mass Psychology of Fascism*, he declared war on the patriarchal and conservative family which he saw as being at the core of mass conservatism: "From the standpoint of social development," Reich wrote, "the family cannot be considered the basis of the authoritarian state, only as one of the most important institutions which support it." The traditional family is a "central reactionary germ cell, the most important place of reproduction of the reactionary and conservative individual. Being itself caused by the authoritarian system, the family becomes the most important institution for its conservation."

In the eyes of the neo-Marxist affection, both romanticism and traditional family values were obstacles to socialist reform and Reich's vehicle towards the new world order was ... orgasm! In his 1927 study, The Function of the Orgasm, he came to the conclusion that: "there is only one thing wrong with neurotic patients: the lack of full and repeated sexual satisfaction." In the hands of Reich, the Marx-Freud hybrid was leading to what some critical cynics dubbed "genital utopia."

Reich believed that for women within the patriarchal society, sex was within the realm of duty and/or restricted to procreation. "The maintenance of the authoritarian family institution requires more than economic dependence of wife and children on husband and father. This dependence can be tolerated only under the condition that the consciousness of being a sexual being is extinguished as far as possible in women and children. The woman is not supposed to be a sexual being, only the producer of children."[36]

Within the traditional society, the woman was robbed of any libidinal consciousness: "This idealization of motherhood is essentially a means of keeping women from developing a sexual consciousness and from breaking through the barriers of sexual repression, of keeping alive their sexual anxieties and guilt feelings. The very existence of woman as a sexual being would threaten authoritarian ideology; her recognition and social affirmation would mean its collapse."[37] Women were mere baby factories, who had only an instrumental role because: "Imperialistic wars require that there be no rebellion in the women against the function that is imposed

---

36. The Mass Psychology of Fascism, Wilhelm Reich pg 56
37. Ibid pg' 56

on them, that of being nothing but child-bearing machines."
This description of the woman and the family fits the
traditional Jewish orthodox family rather better than, say,
the German, French, Italian or Spanish family cell.

But Wilhelm Reich wasn't only a dialectic social
revolutionary, he was also a pragmatist. He invented the
Orgone Energy Accumulator, a wooden box about the size
of a telephone booth, lined with metal and insulated with
steel wool.   The Orgone itself was a vague concept:
an esoteric energy, a universal life force that was massless
yet omnipresent and *promised to* charge up the body with
the life force that circulated in the atmosphere and which
he christened "orgone energy." His Orgone box promised
to improve "orgastic potency" and, by extension, physical
and mental health. Thus, the newly liberated Western
subject was invited to experience the true meaning of
Marx and Freud through sweating towards full
emancipation by means of accumulating 'Orgone energy'
in this wooden box.

Those who watched Woody Allen's comedy film *Sleeper*
(1973) probably remember the Orgasmatron – the orgasm
inducing machine. In Allen's satirical take on Reich's Orgone
box, it is actually the authoritarian regime that encourages
its citizens to emancipate themselves by means of their
genitalia. In Allen's prophetic movie, the orgasm, like
consumerism is a reward from the oppressive regime that
diverts the masses' attention from their existential misery.

The 'authoritarian' Germans, both fascist and communist,
quickly expelled Reich from their ranks. By 1934, even

Freud didn't want anything to do with Reich. The progressive Americans however, tolerated his ideas, at least for a while. Reich was eventually arrested and died in an American prison leaving behind some radical minds, still convinced that the Orgone box was acting as a greenhouse for cosmic, libidinal energy.

Within the free-ranging pornographic realm in which we live, the universe has become an extended Orgone container: pornography is free to all; genital sex is deemed almost Victorian; heterosexuality, at a certain stage, was on the verge of becoming a marginal adventure. And yet authoritarianism hasn't disappeared. Quite the opposite; to borrow Marx's metaphor - it is sex and pornography rather than religion that have become the opium of the masses. And yet, this 'progressive' universe in which we live didn't defeat the inclination towards violence. We are killing millions by proxy in the name of moral interventionism and Coca Cola.

Was Wilhelm Reich a *Mofo*?

When Wilhelm Reich was ten years old, his parents hired tutors to prepare him for the Gymnasium entrance exams. According to Reich, his mother had an affair with one of his tutors and the young Reich became jealous. Reich later claimed that he briefly thought of blackmailing his mother to have sex with him, otherwise he would tell his father about the affair. Eventually Reich confided in his father, who reacted harshly. In 1910, after a protracted period of beatings from his father, his mother committed suicide, a consequence for which Reich blamed himself.

That such an influential man, one who claimed a major role in the sexual liberation of western women and children, had such a problematic 'beginning' interested me and led me to look into the origin of his Oedipal saga.

The person who brought attention to this disturbing affair was Myron Sharaf, an American psychotherapist and a Harvard academic. Sharaf was a student, patient, and colleague of Reich's from 1948 to 1954. He is also the author of what is widely regarded as the definitive biography of Wilhelm Reich, *Fury on Earth* (1983).

On reading Sharaf's account of Reich's blackmail fantasy, my conclusions are more disturbing even than the alleged incident (which I doubt actually occurred).

The manner by which the affair came to light is itself rather peculiar. In late 1919 or early 1920, when Reich was about twenty-three and already a practicing analyst within Freud's circle, Reich wrote his first published article, *The Breakthrough of the Incest Taboo in Puberty.* In this article, Reich reported on a patient who illustrated certain psychological patterns. However, according to Sharaf there is little doubt that the 'patient' described was in fact, Reich himself, especially since many years later Reich "told his elder daughter that the article was a self-analysis."[38]

This is a troubling revelation. First, young Reich publishes a fabricated patient account in a scientific magazine. This is

38. Myron Sharaf: *Fury on Earth*, pg 40

discrediting enough, but there is something else which Sharaf fails to emphasise. At the time, Reich was under the spell of Sigmund Freud. This suggests that Reich might have actually fabricated a patient's account to verify or validate the Oedipal complex, a complex that was practically invented by his mentor. So, while scientists and academics attempt to form theories that correspond with reality and facts, Reich, a member of the Freud cult, apparently reversed the scientific method, contriving 'facts' to correspond with a theory.

Fiddling with facts is a common communist strategy. In one of the early post-revolution Russian jokes, a worker within the Soviet Institute of Marxist Research points out to his superior that the statistics do not fit with the theory. The communist head of the department answers immediately, "so change the numbers so they fit with the theory." By now we can interpret the realistic joke. If the Left ideology is shaped and structured like a dream, then the role of the ideologist is to sustain the slumber. It exists to make sure no one wakes up. Fiddling with facts is apparently the safest way forward.

According to Sharaf, Reich never referred to his first article in his later writings, nor did he speak of it. Though Reich included the article in his bibliography, "his attitude toward this publication was clearly different from his attitude toward other early writings that he would frequently cite or mention."[39] This is not surprising since Reich probably felt guilty about his outrageous academic misconduct.

---

39. Ibid pg 41

To turn to the probably fraudulent academic text itself, Reich declares that he is presenting the case because "it illustrates in an unusually clear way the breakthrough of incestuous wishes into consciousness in puberty." In the article, Reich describes his patient as a twenty-year-old man, a student at a technical school who had sought analysis because he suffered from states of depression and a tendency to ruminate, through which he would make a big deal out of little, insignificant things. Reich, the purported analyst, writes that the patient broke off treatment after four weeks; at precisely the point where the patient had to verbalize certain painful events that had occurred in puberty.

Reich urged the patient to send the analyst a letter describing in writing what he could not say in person. The patient complied and provided a written account of the incident. In the letter, Reich allegedly described his own ordeal.

"This state of affairs lasted about three months. Their meeting (the tutor and the mother) always took place after lunch and was limited to a few minutes. I did not think of the possibility of a sexual relationship. But one day I also became certain about that. Father had gone away at about six o'clock. Mother had again gone to N's (the Tutor's name) room and remained there a very long time. I waited the whole time outside the room, struggling with the decision whether to intrude or to tell father. A vague something held me back. When mother emerged from the room, with blushed cheeks and an erratic, unsteady look, then I knew that it had happened..."[40]

Soon Oedipus is revealed. Reich describes the vivid echoes of the sound of his mother's intercourse with his tutor. He remembered his wish "to plunge into the room" but he was held back by the thought that the loving couple could have killed him. "I had read somewhere that lovers get rid of any intruder," Reich wrote on his fabricated patient's account. But then our liberator found out that his mother celebrating her sexuality actually turned him on to the point that he wanted to blackmail his mother to have sex with him.

"So it went, night after night; always I slipped back and waited till morning. Gradually I became used to it! The horror disappeared and erotic feelings won the upper hand. And then the thought came to me to plunge into the room, and to have intercourse with my mother with the threat that if she didn't I would tell my father."

After this description, Reich abruptly summarises the so-called patient's report: "The father apparently discovered it, and the mother committed suicide by taking poison."

We will never know for sure whether Reich considered sleeping with his mother or forcing her to sleep with him. We will never know whether Reich's mother had sex with the tutor, or with her son. We will never know whether Reich reported the affair to his father and whether it was that action that led to his mother's suicide. However, if Sharaf is correct, then Reich fabricated a patient's account in a

---

40. Ibid pg' 42

scientific magazine which gave evidential weight to his master's Oedipal Theory. Shockingly, Harvard University professor Myron Sharaf is unalarmed by this possible falsification, a response which may well exemplify the drifting away within American academia from the Athenian ethos of truth.

Apparently, fabricating patient reports was a common practice within the Freudian circles. Some even suspect the validity of Freud's patients' reports, all leading to the suspicion that Freud invented dreams to interpret in support of his theories. Could it be that writing and re-writing one's own narrative is, to a certain extent, a modern practice in slight-of-hand persuasion? In fact, Israeli historian Shlomo Sand's reading of contemporary Jewish history suggests that, in the late 19th century, Jews even 'invented' themselves as a nation, a relatively benign fantasy in comparison with the invention of the Oedipal complex that universally attributes to the human infant a libidinal desire towards his or her parents.

While within the Athenian and Germanic world view, truth is defined by correspondence to reality (occasionally with what is conceived to be reality), in the Jerusalemite intellectual realm in which Freud and Reich resided, truth is an elastic notion, shifting and morphing to support one's whims and needs.

But there is a deeper meaning to this story.

In 1950, a collective of premier Frankfurt Institute scholars led by Theodor Adorno joined forces and published *The Authoritarian Personality*. This book defines the authoritarian criteria that contribute towards the emergence of fascist traits. These include conventionalism, authoritarian submission, authoritarian aggression, anti-intellectualism, superstition and stereotypy, power and toughness, projectivity, and exaggerated concerns over sex.

Ironically, all these authoritarian characteristics are apparent in Reich's fraudulent approach. By inventing a patient report to support his master's Oedipal theory, Reich shows himself to be an extreme authoritarian. He meets all the so-called criteria: He is obsessed with sex, reveals aggression, dismisses intellectual integrity, and so on.

But if Reich was an extreme case of an authoritarian personality in 1920, it should be no surprise that a decade or so later Reich blamed the Germans, Italians and Spanish working classes for being authoritarians. In accordance with his master Freud's terminology and method, Reich was projecting his own pathological, authoritarian symptoms onto his neighbours and other European nations.

Science, Religion or Conspiracy

The colossal failure of Marx and dialectical materialism didn't stop Wilhelm Reich from trying to sex-up Marxism in an attempt to sustain its relevance. Reich was entitled to be mistaken; he naively believed that the revolution starts with one good explosive orgasm. Yet, after sixty years of intense 'sex revolution', to blame sexual repression for the rise of conservatism involves a unique state of delusion, intellectual dishonesty or both.

If Leftists are sarcastically defined as 'middle class people who claim to know what is good for working people', progressives and Liberals should be regarded as 'middle class people who are alarmed by working people thinking for themselves.' This was borne out in an article by a contemporary, American, progressive psychoanalyst, Stuart Jeanne Bramhall. "As a long time progressive," Bramhall writes, "I am very alarmed to see low income Americans flock to the reactionary Tea Party and Patriot movement and the ultra-conservative candidates they support."[41]

Bramhall was "amazed to rediscover" that Reich also struggled with this issue. "According to Reich," Bramhall writes, "the strong allure of reactionary politics – and overt fascism – is based in mankind's 6,000 year history of rigid patriarchal, authoritarian and hierarchal social organization, particularly in its effect on childrearing practices."[42] Seemingly, this is about to change, we are all going to be liberated by the G Spot and Bramhall articulates it for us "He (Reich) is actually far more concerned about specific political, religious and economic institutions that deny women and adolescents, in particular, full expression of their sexuality."[43]

Few women are more liberated than American women. For at least three decades in America, both feminists and the LGBTQ movement have been free to promote their message. It is actually the traditional family, the Church and

41. http://www.counterpunch.org/2010/08/06/wilhelm-reich-and-the-tea-party/
42. Ibid
43. Ibid

conservative ideologies that are on the defensive within the contemporary American cultural milieu. And yet, the working classes in the land of the free are becoming more nationalist and patriotic. Despite Bramhall's approval of Reich's theories, the Tea Party grew into a popular grassroots movement.[44] Seemingly, women's liberation didn't stop 'reactionary' Trump from winning the presidential election in 2016. In fact, it was actually white women who overwhelmingly preferred Trump, despite his misogynistic reputation, rather than female, Democratic candidate Hillary Clinton.

One may question how a set of ludicrous, conspiratorial, pseudo-ideologies, foreign to scientific methodical thinking and resembling no form of intellectual contemplation, have become influential cults and even popular religions. What was it in Reich's abstractions on sexual repression that made him into the prophet of the so-called sex revolution? And how, one may also wonder, did Frankfurt School philosopher Herbert Marcuse and his 'infantile' 'Eros and Civilization' (as Erich Fromm labels it), become the spiritual leader of the 1968 student revolution?

Marcuse focused on resolving the Freudian conflict between the Reality Principle (work orientated and leisure less) and the Pleasure Principle (Eros). According to him, the conflict was between alienated labour and Eros. Sex, he insisted is allowed for those in power, namely the capitalists,

---

44. Regardless of the funds the Tea Party is receiving from different oligarchs such as the Koch Brothers.

and was for workers only when it did not disturb their performance. Marcuse contended that in a proper socialist world we will manage without the performance of the "poor" and without a strong suppression of our sexual drives. In his universe, "non-alienated libidinal work" will replace "alienated labour."

Marcuse has managed to liberate some Europeans; a few of his '68 female disciples, now grannies, still expose their breasts on the French Riviera. (I am not going to complain about that). His enthusiastic endorsement of non-genital sex as the highest form of embodiment of the pleasure principle[45] has matured into a very forceful global LGBTQ movement. Yet none of these 'accomplishments' have advanced one jot the 'socialist dream.' On the contrary, these theories have fractured and alienated the working people and limited their ability to resist Mammonism and corporate aggression.

The question needs answering: how could such a bunch of unfounded and clumsily articulated thoughts make it into the ethos of a generation and become the mantra of a cultural revolution?

To address this question, let's first examine the father figure of that school of thought, Dr. Freud himself. While Freud's assumptions regarding human nature and

---

45 Marcuse saw narcissism and homosexuality as "examples of revolutionary sexualities which resisted the restriction of Eros to procreative sexuality." He championed 'polymorphous perversity,' a sexuality not narrowly focused on any specific object or activity. http://newpol.org/content/left-wing-homosexuality-emancipation-sexual-liberation-and-identity-politics

unconsciousness tell us little about human nature or the unconscious, they do help to illuminate Freud's personal obsessions.

As Professor Kevin B. MacDonald suggested in his invaluable book, *The Culture of Critique: An Evolutionary Analysis of Jewish Involvement in Twentieth-Century Intellectual and Political Movements* (1998), the theoretical attempt to reduce love, intimacy and compassion to merely (sexual) 'drives' suggests that Freud and his cult of avid disciples had severe deficits on the human side. The idea that love between mother and son involves an 'oedipal complex' – a murderous intent on the infant's part, is not only troubling, it also has never been scientifically verified. Freud was also wrong about gender. His notion of 'penis envy' is widely accepted as laughable. To date, there's no scientific proof of the id[46], ego, or superego. Further, there's no evidence in support of the notion that human development proceeds through oral, anal, phallic, and genital stages.

So why did the West buy *en masse* into this twisted set of pseudo-scientific and unverifiable speculations? The same question must be applied to Marx and his crude misinterpretation of Hegelian dialectics, for Marxism has never worked as a theoretical model, let alone in practice.

But Marx and Freud have been attracting people for decades. There must be something that explains this mass affinity. Theology may provide some insights.

---

46 Scientific proof within this context refers to both lack of correspondence with facts as well as deficiency in consistency and coherence within the theoretical body itself.

The Abrahamic religions are founded on a set of counter-factual premises. The principles that sustain these religions' validity contradict our empirical knowledge. God, for instance, is that which cannot be perceived, captured or fully realised. God is in the realm of the unattainable. Progressive, revolutionary social and political theories always contain elements of the counterfactual, a god-like status, a pre-determined nature that exceeds the attainable. After all, we pray for the revolution, we join the vigils every Monday, yet the revolution never comes. For the revolution is like the Messiah, it is a metaphysical concept.

When one can neither see God nor verify his existence by empirical means, one is left with two options:

1. Drop God (or religion) altogether.

2. Become a true believer, for the less God is attainable the stronger one must believe.

The latter observation has some significant cultural implications. The greater the misery, the more merciful God becomes. The more widespread the deprivation, the more powerful the church becomes. These commonly accepted precepts explain the popularity of the Abrahamic religions amongst the poor and the ill. But it also explains the animosity of the Marxists and the Left toward religion. Since the traditional Left is structured like an Abrahamic religion, the Left seems to feel compelled to compete with the Church for believers.

The Biblical story of Job teaches that the more God fails to deliver, the more intense belief must become. If God puts your belief to a test, you must submit to his will. From an epistemological perspective, belief transcends knowing, reason and factuality. Belief is a mental state, as opposed to scientific theories that correspond with observations and are subject, theoretically at least, to be refuted by facts. The social revolutionary theorists, (Marx, Freud, Marcuse, Reich, Adorno etc.), like religion, find validation in refutation. The less Marx's thought is able to predict events, the more ardent the Marxist disciples are; the less Freud's analytical model corresponds with reality, the more aggressive become the Freudians.

The social revolutionary theories that we discuss here are structured like the Abrahamic religions, but they are also sustained by a system of *ad hoc* supplements. '*Ad hoc* theory' in philosophy of science signifies a solution assigned to resolve a specific irregularity that doesn't fit within a paradigm or contradicts a theoretical scientific prediction.

Marxism is an evolving theory made up of *ad hoc* theories attempting to explain Marxism's inability to explain events, and its complete failure to make predictions.[47] The consequences have been disastrous. The more Marxism evolves, the further it is removed from social reality. Freudianism falls into the same rubric. Like Marxism, it is an ever-expanding body of ad hoc theories that are increasingly detached from human nature.

The ultimate form of theoretical detachment was offered

---

47. This is said in clear reference to 'dialectical determinism' and social evolution: the belief that higher social existence is 'determined' evolutionary by lower social conditions. It is worth mentioning that Marx himself never referred to dialectical determinism.

by the cultural Marxists (Wilhelm Reich, The Frankfurt School, etc.) in their desperate attempt to merge Marx and Freud into an updated phantasmal school of emancipatory studies. In doing so, they moved further away from their intended congregation and ended up locked within a segregated ghetto of obscure critical theories.

In spite of being vague and inaccessible, cultural Marxism is the closest the Left has ever come to attaining a true popular reception in the West. This is easy to explain. While Marxism is grounded in a relatively simple set of principles, cultural Marxism is neither a principle nor is it principled. It is a largely manipulative method that is set to diminish or even dismantle the so-called bourgeois hegemonic culture[48] in favour of an imaginary emancipation.

It should not surprise us that it was the prominent science philosopher Karl Popper[49] who stood firm against the scientific claims of Marxism, Psychoanalysis and the Freudian Left.

Karl Popper saw falsifiability as the crucial demarcation between science and 'pseudo-science.' In order to be scientific, statements or systems must be capable of

---

48. Gramsci contended that bourgeois hegemony was reproduced in cultural life through the media, academia and religious institutions to 'manufacture consent' and legitimacy. The proletarian struggle for control of the means of production, according to Gramsci, could only succeed once an alternative culture replaces the bourgeois cultural hegemony. For Gramsci it was a 'counter-hegemonic' struggle – advancing alternatives to dominant ideas of what is normal and legitimate.

49. I guess that I should mention that Karl Popper was the academic mentor of George Soros who even named his Open Society Institute after Popper's book, The Open Society and its Enemies.

conflicting with possible, or conceivable observations. A theory can be scientific, according to Popper, if, and only if it is capable of being refuted by facts. The scientific is subject to test, and has the potential to be rebutted empirically (by means of observation). But this can never happen with Marx, Freud, Reich and the cultural Marxists. The cultural Marxist theories always morph to fit the facts by means of *ad hoc* theories. When facts are not available, they are just invented as Reich illustrated in fabricating his patient report.

When working people defy Marx's predictions, Freud is called to the rescue (Reich, Neo-Freudians and the Frankfurt School). When psychoanalysis fails to alleviate psychic pain, the pleasure principle becomes the social liberator and the orgasm defeats alienation. When all these theories fall apart, the Austrian psychologist Melanie Klein introduces the good breast vs the bad breast. You just couldn't make it up.

The results of these modes of thought have been devastating for society, resulting in the tyranny of correctness, with ID politics evolving into sectarian battles, and so on. The revolutionary precept is structured like a conspiracy theory. As opposed to an Athens that is obsessed with truth, reason and logos, the Jerusalem cultural Marxism is sustained by an institutional dismissal of the truth and the removal of any method that may result in approaching the truth. The success of a particular conspiracy theory is not defined by a clear correspondence between theory and facts, but by one's willingness to buy into it.

It is the conspiratorial nature of Marxism, Freudianism, cultural Marxism and the New Left that explains not only the popularity of these views amongst those who are inclined towards conspiracy, but also why many progressives are themselves intensely aggressive towards other conspiring minds. And as the Austrian philosopher Otto Weininger taught us, "we hate in others only what we do not wish to be, and what notwithstanding we are partly." The Progressive's animosity towards the conspiratorial is in its essence a radical form of projection.

Bunkers and Meatheads

Americans born in the 1960s and earlier can readily recall that, as far as freedom of thought is concerned, there was a time when America believed itself to be a free place – and they know that it no longer is. Yet most Americans struggle to point out when and how it happened. When did political correctness become a dominant culture? How did ID politics become a universal code?

Archie Bunker is one of America's most beloved TV characters.[50] Archie was the fictional star of the 1970s television sitcom *All in the Family*. This iconic satire, the Stateside copy of the successful British comedy, *Till Death Do Us Part*, told the story of a typical white, patriarchal, working-class family living in the New York City borough of Queens.

---

50. *TV Guide* ranked Archie Bunker number 5 on its 50 Greatest TV Characters of All Time list. In 2005, Archie Bunker was listed as number 1 on the Bravo channel's 100 Greatest TV Characters.

The patriarch was a middle-aged WWII veteran - a narrow-minded, conservative, blue-collar worker and a good Christian, a cherished inhabitant of Hillary Clinton's "basket of deplorables." He was a simple man who brazenly spoke his mind - an early prototype of Donald Trump.

All in the Family's routine was an ongoing quarrel between Archie the 'beloved bigot' and his liberal son-in-law and university student Mike, to whom Archie refers as a "dumb Polack" and "Meathead" for being "dead from the neck up."

The one crucial question Americans may want to ask themselves is, how did it happen that, despite Archie being one of the most beloved characters on American TV, America has become a nation of meatheads, suppressed by the tyranny of correctness and Identitarian sensitivities?

Archie and 'Meathead' agreed on nothing, yet, the nature of their dispute, and the way in which it was delivered, may provide us a window into the liberal cultural strategies that have been implemented in America and the West since the 1960s.

All in the Family succeeded in pushing the liberal agenda into every American living room. The tactics were simple but incredibly forceful. On a weekly basis, it showed the tension between Archie's 'irrational' bigotry and the level-headed liberalism of his son-in-law. Week after week, our most 'beloved bigot' was reduced into a 'reactionary caricature', while 'Meathead' was the voice of liberal transition. The son-in-law character was actually slightly pathetic, an anti-hero protagonist. Yet, for all kinds of reasons, we accepted he had a vision, leading the way 'forward' towards a new form of middle class decency. They say that in America, working class folk like to move up the ladder and Meathead provided them with a possible path.

Humour was the magic glue that bound it all together. To quote progressive Chicago community organiser Saul Alinsky, "humour is essential, for through humour much is accepted that would have been rejected if presented seriously." Back in the 1970s, Norman Lear, the brilliant producer who brought Archie Bunker to life, couldn't just attack white, protestant America or ridicule what they believed to be their social values. Satire was his sword.

Lear was a man with a clear political agenda. Like many progressive Jews at the time, he was a vocal critic of the ideas held by the religious right and was a staunch supporter of secular thought and secularism in general. In 1981, he founded People for the American Way (PFAW). This progressive, advocacy organization opposed the interjection of religion in politics. However, while PFAW's achievements have been limited, Lear's Meathead actually revolutionised America, transforming it into a PC tyranny dominated by ID and group politics. While the FBI and the CIA were desperate to plant agents in what they believed to be subversive political cells, Norman Lear was pushing his own political agenda, leading a cultural revolution that was taking place under their radars – and he did it all with a typewriter.

One may wonder, was Norman Lear a conspiratorial cultural Marxist? Was he a student of Gramsci or Marcuse? I don't know the answers and I don't even care. The crucial lesson here is that cultural manipulation is a sophisticated project that settles in, undetected, under your skin. It is designed to transform your language, your values, and all this while you are unwittingly having beer or popcorn on your sofa, laughing your head off in front of your TV screen.

But there is an interesting twist to this story. In the 1970s Archie Bunker, owing to his being a bag of blind spots, couldn't grasp the transforming reality around him. He didn't see Blacks, Hispanics, feminists, lesbians. He felt secure in his little America in Queens. But nowadays, it is the Meatheads, the progressives, and the liberals who happen to be the bag of blind spots. It is they who haven't been able to comprehend the transforming reality. They weren't listening to the cry of millions of Americans, and they couldn't foresee the defeat of their own identity-based politics. They couldn't see Brexit coming, they couldn't see Trump winning. They were and are detached.

Cultural Capitalism

At the same time that Wilhelm Reich and members of the Frankfurt School were trying to figure out how to utilise Freud and Marx in the service of anti-capitalist emancipatory social change, Freud's nephew Edward Bernays was showing American capitalists and corporations how to brainwash the masses and reduce people into obedient consumers.

Bernays was one of the most powerful and influential people in 20th century America. He is the man who invented the media-spin and the false need and yet, most Americans have never heard of him. They know nothing about the man who shaped their society and dominated their desires.

Born in 1891 in Vienna to Jewish parents, his mother was Sigmund Freud's sister Anna, his father was Ely Bernays, brother of Freud's wife, Martha Bernays.

During the First World War and shortly after, Edward worked for Woodrow Wilson's administration within the Committee on Public Information. Bernays was overwhelmed by the success of the American's war propaganda machine and decided to implement the same tactics in support of big business.

In the 1920s, Bernays reached the conclusion that the plethora of industrially-created goods and ideas, together with the new democratic freedoms, could lead to confusion. His solution was propaganda. "To avoid such confusion, society consents to have its choice narrowed to ideas and objects brought to its attention through propaganda of all kinds."[51] Propaganda, according to Bernays, is there to regulate free-market competition, to 'help' people to choose products and services more calculatedly by their own will. It is, as he claimed, the "executive arm of the invisible government."

For Bernays, the invisible government is that which "dictates our thoughts, directs our feelings and controls our actions." This corporate body is clearly unelected, and in fact just another name for elites and oligarchs: "the intelligent minorities which need to make use of propaganda continuously and systematically ... Only through the active

---

51. *Propaganda : Public Mind in the Making*, pg 11

energy of the intelligent few can the public at large become aware of and act upon new ideas."[52] Propaganda is the medium that restrains democracy and transforms it into a functional enterprise. So, post-Bernays, while people believe themselves to be free, they are, in practice, bound to a limited set of predetermined choices that are decided by the 'invisible government.' In Bernays' universe freedom is an illusion.

Cultural Marxists and the propaganda ideologists appeared to be pushing in completely opposite directions – the cultural Marxists push for anti-authoritarian emancipation, Bernays worked to enslave masses to the capital and market forces – but both subscribed to a similar notion of elitism and mass manipulation. Both interfered with identity and exploited identification. Both saw the people around them simply as guinea pigs in an on-going social experiment.

The cultural Marxists believed that cultural manipulation would lead to a social shift. Bernays points to an identical process within the heart of the capitalist industrial society and asks, "if we understand the mechanism and motives of the group mind, is it not possible to control and regiment the masses according to our will without their knowing it?"[53] His answer seems to be in the affirmative: "The recent practice of propaganda has proved that it is possible, at least up to a certain point and within certain limits."[54]

---

52. Ibid, pg 31
53. Ibid, pg 47
54. Ibid, pg 47

Further, "human desires are the steam which makes the social machine work. Only by understanding them can the propagandist control that vast, loose-jointed mechanism which is modern society."[55] This line of thought was also attributed to Wall Street banker Paul Mazur of Lehman Brothers who, in 1927, claimed "We must shift America from a *needs*, to a *desires* culture," he wrote. "People must be trained to desire, to want new things even before the old had been entirely consumed. We must shape a new mentality in America. Man's desires must overshadow his needs."[56] The transition from need to desire was exactly what made the American economy grow exponentially. The Americans learned to buy new cars before their old ones died. They learned to identify with products and also to be identified by the products they owned.

In his invaluable 2002 BBC documentary *The Century of the Self*, director Adam Curtis focuses on the work of Bernays within the context of the influence of Freud's conception of the unconscious. In the first episode, Curtis argues that Bernays borrowed the concept of irrationality and the unconscious from his Uncle Sigmund. Such an approach to Bernays' work is common but I'm not so sure that this is the case. Bernays' thesis as presented in his 1928 book *Propaganda, Public Mind in the Making*, is not based on psychoanalytical scholarship and not related to the Freudian paradigm. The manipulative strategies offered by the book suggest that the masses'

---

55. Ibid, pg 52
56. *The Century of the Self*, 2002 BBC documentary by Adam Curtis

behaviours could be actually rationalized and manipulated accordingly. He clearly diagnosed some weak spots in human nature – and he knew how to translate them into capital. It wasn't peoples' unconscious or irrationality that Bernays was dealing with, it was the desire – the conscious sense of becoming, that vivid awareness of the self, wanting to transcend into something else, to be rich, to be attractive, to be *special* or in Lacanian terms, to be the desire of the other.[57]

So I don't think Bernays was a follower of Freud. Bernays was a cultural capitalist. Dominating others' desires was his recipe for making money. He was a uniquely gifted, non-ethical capitalist whose ideas were as simple and consistent as they were devastating, a master in creating false needs and breaking taboos.

One of his most famous campaigns was the women's cigarette-smoking campaign in the 1920s when he helped the tobacco industry overcome one of the biggest social taboos of the time: women smoking in public. At the time, women were only allowed to smoke, if at all, in designated areas. Bernays staged the 1929 Easter Parade in New York City, showing models holding lit Lucky Strike cigarettes, or "Torches of Freedom" as he called them. Following Bernays, what seemed as a laudable campaign for gender equality translated into millions of new female

---

57. For Jacques Lacan, 'desire is the desire of the Other.' Lacan maintained throughout his career that desire is the desire to be desirable i.e. being an object of desire in the eyes of others. This observation explains human behavior. It explains why women spend hours in front of mirrors and why boys love new big cars.

consumers for the tobacco industry. It is reasonable to argue that Bernays, the cultural capitalist, in his realization that identity and identification can be utilized politically and financially, was way ahead of the cultural Marxists.

Edward Bernays convinced the industry that it was the news, not advertising, that was the best medium to carry their message to an unsuspecting public. After all, news comes free, it spreads widely and, most important, it is believed. As such, "Torches of Freedom" was presented as news – which it certainly was not – yet the impact on the relevant market was immediate.

Was he a deviously conspiratorial character? Not really. Like so many others in this book, he did it all in the open. In fact, he openly proclaimed his exceptionalist views in his 1928 book. Is there a philosophical continuum between Bernays, Wilhelm Reich, Adorno, Marcuse and Norman Lear? The answer is yes. We are dealing with elitists' cultural manipulative paradigms, designed to change people and society. The cultural shifters, Bernays, Reich, Marcuse and Lear were not elected politicians, they were not public figures, they were intellectuals for whom all you needed to change the world was a typewriter.

By the clarity and the power of his thought, Bernays managed to boost the American economy and enslave the masses. His list of clients included President Calvin Coolidge, Procter & Gamble, CBS, the United Fruit Company, the American Tobacco Company, General Electric, Dodge Motors, the CIA and others. But here again, comes a twist. When white and blue collar Americans voted for Donald

Trump and his motto, "Make America Great Again," it was the Bernays' universe for which they were nostalgic. In the ultra-capitalist world created by propaganda, there was an authoritarian, elitist order dictated by an 'invisible government.' Freedom was largely an illusion, but labour and manufacturing were for real. In Bernays' universe, people woke up in the morning to go to work just to accumulate enough money to purchase things they didn't need.

I guess Americans still want to buy things they don't need. It's just the cash to do so which they lack.

Unskewing the Polls

Just three days ahead of the 2016 American presidential election, the *Huffington Post* criticised political opinion survey website *538*'s star pollster Nate Silver for "Unskewing polls in Trump's direction," for suggesting that a Trump victory was a realistic possibility. Ryan Grim wrote: "*HuffPost* Pollster is giving Clinton a 98 percent chance of winning, and the *New York Times*' model at The Upshot puts her chances at 85 percent. There is one outlier, however, that is causing waves of panic among Democrats around the country and injecting Trump backers with the hope that their guy might pull this thing off after all. Nate Silver's *538* model gives Donald Trump a heart-stopping 35% chance of winning as of this weekend."[58] The *Huffington Post* went so far as to accuse Silver of "making a mockery of the very forecasting industry that he popularized."

In perspective, Nate Silver and his *538* were obviously spot on. Donald Trump won the election. The *Huffington Post* and the *New York Times* were totally off the mark. Is this a coincidence?

How is it possible that the Democratic Party and the mainstream media have managed to totally miss the level of anger that unites the American masses and blue-collar workers in particular? These questions go far beyond polling strategy or the science of statistics. We are dealing with a state of aloofness that verges on institutional detachment.

The following story may throw light on this peculiar political phenomenon intrinsic to progressive and liberal politics. On the 9th of November, the morning that followed Hillary Clinton's humiliating defeat, the *Washington Post* revealed that Hillary and her campaign relied heavily on an algorithm named Ada. Ada was Clinton's secret weapon. "It is a complex computer algorithm that the campaign was prepared to publicly unveil after the election as its invisible guiding hand".[59] Named after a female 19th-century mathematician — Ada, Countess of Lovelace — "the algorithm was said to play a role in virtually every strategic decision

---

58 http://www.huffingtonpost.com/entry/nate-silver-election-forecast_us_581e1c33e4b0d9ce6fbc6f7f

59. https://www.washingtonpost.com/amphtml/news/post-politics/wp/2016/11/09/clintons-data-driven-campaign-relied-heavily-on-an-algorithm-named-ada-what-didnt-she-see/?client=safari

Clinton aides made, including where and when to deploy the candidate and her battalion of surrogates and where to air television ads — as well as when it was safe to stay dark."

Ada ran 400,000 simulations a day of what the race against Trump might look like. It provided a "detailed picture of which battleground states were most likely to tip the race in one direction or another"

What is astonishing in this story is that neither Hillary Clinton nor her campaign managers, who were so attuned to Ada, managed to hear the cry of the American people. They failed to see the despair in Michigan or the fatigue in Pennsylvania. I guess that the answer is that Ada must have been a 'liberal' algorithm and as flawed as the virus-infected party it was created to serve. The fetish for 'science and technology' replaced the ability to be empathic and human, to read the American public accurately. This is the true story behind Clinton and the Democratic Party's defeat.

By now we should be able to grasp this detachment. The liberal and progressive outlooks are constructed as a dream. They envision the world as it ought to be. In practice, progressives and liberals don't simply forget what the world is, they often have invested in hiding the truth from themselves.

Hillary Clinton and her campaign, just like the *New York Times*, the *Guardian* and the *Huffington Post*, were in a complete state of denial. Boasting with righteous hubris, they failed to read the map. Rather than meeting the voters and grasping their needs, they preferred to consult with

Ada. Tragically, this failure is institutional. It is embedded in progressive and liberal thought.

On a positive note and within the context of universal and Christian thought, progressives are people who advocate social change, improvement and reforms of the social order, as opposed to wishing to maintain things as they are. But progressives often believe that those who don't agree with them are a bunch of 'reactionaries.' It is this binary differentiation between 'us' (the 'force of good') and 'them' (the 'deplorables') that makes progressive politics into a secular manifestation of 'chosenness.' This may explain why progressive and liberal politics often evolve into an arrogant and exceptionalist worldview. One may wonder whether the resemblance between progressive exceptionalism and Jewish secular chosenness is mere coincidence or whether the link between the two has some historical, cultural and ideological depth to it.

Yuri Slezkine and The Jewish Century

"The Jews, however, are beyond all doubt the strongest, toughest, and purest race at present living in Europe; they know how to succeed even under the worst conditions (in fact better than under favourable ones) by means of virtues of some sort, which one would like nowadays to label as vices – owing above all to a resolute faith which does not need to be ashamed before modern ideas..." -Friedrich Nietzsche[60]

---

60. *Beyond Good and Evil*, Friedrich Nietzsche, chapter 8

Yuri Slezkine's *The Jewish Century* was published in 2006. The book revolutionised the scholarly attitude to Jewish history, culture and politics. Slezkine's thesis was straightforward: The modern age is a Jewish age – all other people are, to varying degrees, similar to the Jews. According to the American history professor, Jews adapted to the New World better than many or even any other groups, they have become the mark of enlightenment, the premier symbol and standard of modern life everywhere.

The Jewish Century was cherished by both Jews and by so-called anti-Semites. Jews loved the book and its author for its scholarly confirmation that they have been prominent within the Western world culturally, politically, intellectually, ideologically and so on. But the so-called anti-Semites also loved Slezkine's work for the same reason, it confirmed that which they had been arguing all along about Jewish dominance.

Slezkine's work was an invaluable contribution to the study of the 20th century. It also had a significant influence on my work and my approach towards Jewish ID politics. It is hardly a secret that some of my critics complain that I 'see a Jew in everything and everyone.' This is not entirely true. I do not care about ethnicity, biology or race, but I do care about ideology, ID politics and culture. I see the cultural and ideological impact of Jerusalem on pretty much every aspect of Western life. But, unlike most commentators, I allow myself to voice my criticism of that aspect.

From this point I will delve into a study of Jewish ID politics within the context of the post-political condition. We will try to identify the ideological ethos that shaped the cultural Marxist project as well as its opposition. We will identify the depth of 'chosenness' within progressive and liberal thought. If, as Slezkine suggests, Jews are the bearers of the new world, we may want to understand what is it about Jewish culture, ideology and survival tactics that introduced such powerful social developments.

Judaism and Other Jewish Religions

Many scholars, in their attempt to understand Jewish politics, Jewish revolutionary ideologies, Jewish culture and lobbying, Zionism and Israeli politics, attribute significant importance to Judaism and the Talmud. Some Jewish progressives insist that it is a Jewish 'humanist heritage' that is the driving force behind all those so-called Tikkun Olam mantras. I am troubled by this approach. As much as Judaism and the Talmud contain some exceptionalist and racist elements, the crimes committed by the Jewish state, for instance, are largely perpetrated by a secular community, people for whom Judaic religious thought is foreign and who have little knowledge of the contents of the Talmud. The same can be said about Marx, Freud, Reich and most of the Frankfurt School researchers, except Erich Fromm who was a rabbinical student. Most Jewish intellectuals and revolutionaries were raised in relatively secular Jewish environments that simply did not include Talmudic study.

But Judaism is just one Jewish religion. As the study of Jewish identity politics and Jewish political power emerges, it becomes clear that those who identify as Jews, subscribe to many different, and even contradictory views, ideologies and spiritual insights of which Judaism is only one amongst many. An attempt to list the contemporary precepts held by Jews, conveys a clear image of ideological, spiritual and intellectual diversity.

If Judaism is just one Jewish religion amongst many, then Judaism and the Talmud cannot be regarded as the DNA of Jewish tribalism or exceptionalism. It could be the other way around – Judaism and the Talmud may simply be symptoms of Jewish tribal identity. In other words, it is not the Jew that is formed by the Judaic text, it is the Judaic text that is formed by the Jew.

Such an approach – a reversal of the cause and effect relationship – could lead to a Copernican revolution in our understanding of Judaism, Jewish ID politics, Zionism, Jewish revolutionary theories, *Tikkun Olam* and even the meaning of the Jewish state.

Judaism and the Talmud may not be at the root of 'chosenness' or tribal supremacy. Instead, it may be that the Talmud is a by-product of Judeo-centric, exilic tribal orientation. The Jewish exceptionalist inclination may in fact predate the Judaic chauvinist text.

Since the French Revolution and the emancipation of European Jewry, Jews have been fleeing the rigid Rabbinical and Talmudic universe. They have been breaking down the ghetto walls in search for new meaning. Many attempted to cleanse themselves of their old identity and assimilate into their host nations.

Countless Jews achieved this goal and have disappeared into the crowd and lost all traces of Jewish tribalism. However, many Jews have drifted away from the Torah and the Talmud, yet maintained a close affinity with Jewish tribal thinking. Without necessarily being aware that they have done so, they have retained a strong spiritual bond with their tribal ideological roots and philosophy.

We will try to identify the characteristics of the Jewish religious spirit at the heart of different politics and ideologies. Two centuries of Jewish assimilation, secularisation and nationalism have made it clear that almost every ideology or thought can be transformed into a 'Jewish religion.' But what is this malleable Jewish religion?

Let's examine a partial list of competing ideas often professed by Jews to be their contemporary belief system:

Judaism – The core and oldest religious belief of the Jewish people. Apparently not overwhelmingly popular amongst Jews anymore.

Atheism – The belief that abolition of religion altogether is good for the Jews as well as for everyone else.

The Holocaust – The belief in the primacy of Jewish suffering. The Holocaust is considered the most popular 'Jewish religion' at the time this book is being written.[61]

Free Market - The belief that the free market is good for the Jews as well as most rich people (Milton Friedman[62]).

---

61. It may seem outrageous to refer to the Holocaust as a Jewish religion. But as we will see later, more than just a few Jewish scholars insist that this is indeed the case.

62. Capitalism and The Jews, Milton Friedman, https://fee.org/articles/

Marxism – The belief that middle class people know what is good for the working class.

Neo-Marxism (aka Frankfurt School) – The assumption that cultural manipulation is the way forward as long as the Goyim don't notice.

Feminism – The belief that women's liberation from the male yoke is good for both women and men.

Psychoanalysis – The belief that everybody could do with a shrink.

Political Correctness – The belief that self-censorship is the cheapest and most effective means to paralyze everyone who isn't a Zionist.

ID Politics – The belief that the personal is political unless you are Muslim or White.

Human Rights – The belief that human rights are good for everyone except the Palestinians and anti-Zionists (Alan Dershowitz & Co.)

Pro-immigration – The belief that mass immigration diverts attention from the Jews and also weakens the cohesiveness of 'White' working people.

Anti-immigration – The belief that immigration turns London into 'Londonistan' (according to the Zionist journalist Melanie Philips) and this is very bad for the Jews.

Cultural Marxism – the belief that a cultural shift rather than actual proletarian revolution will move society forward (The Frankfurt School, Wilhelm Reich)

Alt-Right – the belief that cultural Marxism is a modern

capitalism-and-the-jews/

day evil formed to obliterate 'Judeo-Christian values' (Andrew Breitbart, David Horowitz)

Tikkun Olam – The belief that Jews know how to make the world into a better place (cultural Marxism, Frankfurt School, Rabbi Michael Lerner).

Anti-War, Anti-Zionism – The belief that Zionist wars are very bad for the Jews in particular (Philip Weiss, Jewish Voice for Peace, Noam Chomsky etc.)

Pro-War, Moral Interventionism & Neo-conservatism – The belief that the English-speaking Empire fighting for Israel is not such a bad idea after all.

Early Zionism – The view that schlepping Jews to Palestine is good for everyone (Jews as well the Goyim).

Contemporary Zionism – A Holocaust shelter as well as a safe haven for diaspora Jews and the Russian oligarchy's Mammon.

Cosmopolitanism – The belief that everyone except Jews should shake off any sense of rootedness, patriotism, nationalism or any other feeling that may involve orientation.

One may be amused by the above list. It is deliberately presented in a humorous manner. In fact, this kind of sarcasm is typical of Jewish humour. It puts into play a moderated form of self-deprecation – it is the manner by which Jews own their cultural symptoms.

But the list is absurd. Some of the precepts contradict each other. Judaism and atheism seem to be in complete opposition. Anti-war sentiment, as preached by a few vocal Jewish voices on the Left as the 'true meaning of Jewish universalist heritage,' is in clear conflict with the wars pushed by the forceful Zionist neocons who preach moral interventionism in the name of their Jewishness (Bernard-Henri Lévy). Zionism, regarded by many Jews as the contemporary embodiment of Jewish spiritual practice, is also opposed by a few Jews who insist that Jewish anti-Zionism is the true spiritual meaning of their Jewish existence.

These disparate views illustrate that polarity and contradiction are inherent in Jewish culture and politics. Jews can simultaneously lead both the capitalist world and the socialist revolution. Jews can unite to accomplish the Zionist dream while other Jews strive to delegitimise Zionism in the 'name of the Jewish people.' Jews can dominate both Wall Street financial markets as well as the Wall Street occupation movements that call to dismantle that symbolic centre of Mammonism. In short, Jews can simultaneously claim to represent the 99% while being the 1%.

If Jews can so adeptly lead both sides of an issue, then what is it that makes a precept or a belief system into a particularly Jewish one? What leads Jews to identify collectively with a particular idea or perception? Or, in short, how do we define a Jewish religion?

Being Chosen

In order for a realm of thought to qualify as a Jewish pseudo-religion, it must provide a context for chosenness. All Jewish religions without exception facilitate exceptionalism-entangled-with-righteousness.

In 2007, while so many high-level neocon Jews were

promoting war, I came across an announcement about the formation of a lobbying group called 'Jews against the War.' These 'anti' war Jews opposed war in the name of their Jewishness and referred at the time to the "Jewish community's long history of standing up for social justice and human rights."[63] It seems as if both the 'pro' and 'anti' war Jews manage to reaffirm their unique Jewish identity by supporting opposing political goals. One way to resolve this peculiar tension is to accept that love does not obey the rules of logic, and Jewish self-love is no exception.

In the 1970-80s a few prominent Israeli philosophers such as Professors Yeshayahu Leibowitz and Adi Ophir[64] were amongst the first to realise that the Holocaust had become a Jewish religion. The Holocaust, they noted, has its priests and prophets, its commandments and dogmas. It has its rituals, official celebrations (memorial) days and even a pilgrimage. American historian Norman Finkelstein later explored the entire industry that has attached itself to the Holocaust. In fact, the legendary Israeli diplomat Abba Eban foresaw Finkelstein's argument in the 1950s with the humorous adage 'there is no business like Shoah business.'

Crucially, the Holocaust affirms the uniqueness of its followers. It is devoted to the primacy of Jewish suffering, granting the Jew the crown of thorns as the ultimate sufferer. It is also used to justify every Jewish action, from ethnic cleansing to genocide. And every psychoanalyst can confirm

---

63. https://www.indymedia.org/de/2007/03/882372.shtml

64. Adi Ophir - *On Sanctifying the Holocaust: An Anti-Theological Treatise, in Tikkun,* volume 2, issue 1, pg 61 to 67

that often the abused becomes an abuser. In order to affirm the primacy of Jewish suffering, the Holocaust must maintain the uniqueness and righteousness of the Jew.

The atheist derives his 'special' status by being 'liberated' from any 'irrational' thought or 'medieval ritual.' Marx transforms from an intellectual icon into a religious father figure when the 'Marxist' becomes the chosen 'vehicle' towards universal justice. Psychoanalysis becomes a Jewish religion by elevating its followers into the authors of their own biographies.

In sum, for a concept to work as a Jewish religion it must provide a clear exceptionalist context.

Jewish Religions and the Prospect of Dissent

"The Jewish religion is a religion of Mitzvoth (commandments) and without this religious idiom, the Jewish religion doesn't exist at all." Professor Yeshayahu Leibowitz

While Islam and Christianity are belief systems, Judaism is an obedience-regulatory system. The Judaic universe is ruled by 'mitzvoth,' a set of 613 precepts and 'directives' thought to have been ordered by God.

In opposition to Christianity and Islam that build from spiritual and heavenly precepts in worship to a transcendental god, the Judaic subject subscribes to strict earthly and material observance. While the Islamo-Christian is wrapped in God's love and the spirituality of the sublime and divinity, the follower of Judaism is judged by his or her ability to adhere to hundreds of rigorous earthly orders.

A brief look at the Judaic daily Shema Prayer[65] reveals the nature of Judaism as an obedience regulatory system. In Judaism, even God-loving is not voluntary:

"You shall love Adonai your God with all your heart, with all your soul, and with all your might. Take to heart these instructions with which I charge you this day.

...Thus you shall remember to observe all my commandments and to be holy to your God. I am Adonai, your God, who brought you out of the land of Egypt to be your God: I am Adonai your God."

(*Shema Prayer* from *Deuteronomy and Numbers*)

For the Jew, belief and God-loving are not subject to either rational discretion or spiritual impulse. God loving, as we read above, is a strict charge, an order.

A look at the work of Maimonides (Rabbi Moshe ben Maimon), the medieval Jewish philosopher who was the most prolific and influential Torah scholar of the Middle Ages, reveals that 'believing in God' is, defined by him as the very first mitzvah, a primary commandment or duty as opposed to an involuntary act or an impulse that is inspired by worship.[66]

But if Judaism is not exactly a belief system, what is

---

65. The Shema is one of only two prayers that are specifically commanded in the Torah. It is the oldest fixed daily prayer in Judaism, recited morning and night since ancient times.

66. It is worth mentioning that Maimonides' decision to make belief in God into a first mitzvah came under sharp criticism by numerous Rabbis along the years.

it? Does the Judaic subject believe in anything at all?

The answer is yes: the Jew believes in 'The Jews' and the Jews believe in 'The Jew.' This mutual affirmation establishes a solid and forceful tribal continuum that serves the collective as well as the singular subject. Accordingly, each adheres to the collective and vice versa. In pragmatic terms, the Jew sticks to the 'chosen people' and, together, the 'chosenites' uphold a collective sense of chosenness. This state of affairs may help us to grasp the Jewish inclination towards segregation and the fear of assimilation that was explored by many of the early Zionists.

In Judaic orthodoxy, chosenness is the belief that the Jewish people were singularly chosen to enter into a covenant with God. For religious Jews, being chosen is realised as a duty. According to Judaic belief, the Jews have been placed on earth to fulfil a certain purpose. God bestowed this purpose on the Jews and they pass it down from father to son.

It does seem possible that the first Jews invented a God who chose them over all other people. This God is occasionally cruel, often non-ethical and not a nice father. The Jewish God doesn't even allow his people to utter his name. One may wonder what led the first Jews to conjure such a horrid father figure. Why did they sustain their relationship with such an obnoxious father? Mostly, they didn't. And while they don't believe in God, they are observant of God. They believe in themselves: the Jews believe in 'The Jew.'

Within this peculiar, troubled family affair, the Jew is free to dump God (as many have, especially in the last two centuries), as an author can freely rewrite or at least reshape his or her own narrative. But only rarely does the Jew dump the Jews. That is the essence of the tribal bond. Assimilated Jews may leave God behind, they become atheists and secularists, but they never leave the tribe.

And what about God, can he be emancipated, can he choose another people? Certainly not. Unlike the Jew who is free to dump God while clinging to a new Jewish identity, the tribe, the blood, the matzah balls, or even Marx or Trotsky, the Jewish God is a mere Jewish protagonist. He can't go anywhere, he is stuck with 'his' chosen people for eternity.

Chosenness, so it seems, is hardly a heavenly gift, it is more in the nature of a curse. It confines the Jew to a ghetto of self-imposed commandments. Instead of beauty, holiness and the pursuit of the divine and the sublime, the rabbinical Jew is left with an earthly obedience scheme sustained by a rigid tribal setting. 'The Jew' and 'The Jews' are bound in a set of mutual affirmations in which God serves an instrumental role.

This adamantine bond between the collective and the individual is essential for an understanding of the dichotomy between Judaic tribalism and the universal appeal of Islamo-Christian beliefs.

Basket of Deplorables

For the Islamo-Christian, secularisation entails a rejection of the transcendental, i.e. a failure to believe in a divine god.

But for the rabbinical Jew, failure to conform constitutes a rejection of the Jews as a whole, crudely interfering with the binary relationship between 'The Jew' and 'the Jews.' It shatters that self-affirming mechanism. While in the case of Christianity or Islam, rejection of the Almighty puts the unbeliever's soul at risk, in the case of Judaism, an act of rejection is a repudiation of the entire tribe.

This relationship between the Jew and the Jews explains why secular and so-called 'progressive' Jews are often as resistant to dissent or criticism from within, and as obdurate as even the rabbinical Jews. Judaism is a belief system based on obedience and regulation and all other forms of Jewish religion such as Jewish identity politics, Marxism, and the Holocaust religion require the same obedience-regulatory philosophy.

Jews often drop their Gods and invent a new god who 'facilitates' subscription to a new regulatory system. And just like the old, the new system contains a new set of strict commandments, a special vocabulary and rigorous boundaries of 'kosher' conduct.

At the beginning of the 20th century, Bolshevism, with its sense of self-righteousness and adherence to strict rules of obedience, appealed to many Eastern European Jews. Before long, Bolshevism matured into a genocidal doctrine that made Old Testament barbarism look like a child's fairy tale. But most importantly, Bolshevism had a strict atmosphere of party politics, a set of commandments and a prescribed intolerant attitude towards dissenters.

The Holocaust, today's most popular Jewish religion, may

be the ultimate and final stage in Jewish historical development. According to the Holocaust religion; 'God died in Auschwitz[67],' and 'the Jew' is the new Jewish God. The Holocaust religion has united 'The Jew' and 'the Jews' within a self-sufficient, comprehensive and independent 'God-less' narrative. Jews constitute the victims, the oppressors and the redeemers. For example, the Jews transformed slavery into empowerment and they did it all by themselves, in spite of being dumped by their treacherous God.

Like Judaism, the Holocaust religion prescribes a manner of speech and a strict set of commandments. Most crucially, like all other Jewish religions, it is totally and deplorably intolerant of any form of dissent. Any intellectual attempting to challenge the historicity of any aspect of the Holocaust evokes the most severe and humiliating punishments: imprisonment, excommunication, financial pressure and social and even physical harassment.

In the 1970s, Israeli philosopher Yeshayahu Leibowitz commented that Jews may believe in many different things but all Jews believe in the Holocaust. The Holocaust religion represents the culmination of Jewish history and the ultimate bond between 'The Jew' and 'the Jews.'

Discourse can be understood as a set of boundaries outlining the rules of a particular exchange. But the Jewish

---

67. 'God died in Auschwitz' is a sentiment occasionally associated with Elie Wiesel and his bestseller Night. The Jewish Holocaust theologian Richard L. Rubenstein also wrote extensively on the meaning and impact of the Holocaust within the context of Judaism. In his book *After Auschwitz*, Rubenstein argued that the experience of the Holocaust shattered the traditional Judaic concept of God.

religious discourse is better understood as a radical and uncompromising form of intolerance. Jewish religion is a template of differentiation, setting a clear demarcation between the holy (*kodesh*) and the ungodly (*hol*), the *Kosher* (proper) and the *Taref* (improper).

The Jewish religion is very particular in regard to the manner in which it maintains its club and its membership. Accordingly, boycotting and excommunications (*herem*) are ingrained in Jewish religious practice and Judaism has earned itself a terrible reputation in that respect. The appalling treatment of both Uriel Da Costa[68] and Baruch Spinoza provide us with an insight into the Jewish religious phobia of innovation, original thinking and dissent.

Judaism provides a prototypical example of intolerance, but sadly, it is not the only one. There are many other 'Jewish' religions, each with its own brand of intolerance. In order to qualify as a Jewish religion, a precept, idea or a realm of thought must include clear rules of disengagement. Such rules must clearly define who is 'in' and who is 'out', who is 'included' and who is 'excluded.' For Judaism it is the Goyim; the Holocaust has its deniers, the Freudians hate the Jungians and the Behaviorists, the Marxists have the Bourgeoisie, the Zionists have the 'antis' and the 'antis' have the Zionists. And the progressives exclude the White reactionaries, or, shall we just say, all those who voted for Donald Trump.

All Jewish religions separate their followers from the rest

---

68. Uriel Da Costa (1585 – 1640) was a Portuguese Jew who lived in Amsterdam and was heavily punished by the rabbinical institutions for expressing rational dissent to their institutions.

of humankind by setting an exceptionalist template that leads inexorably towards a severe form of detachment. Hillary Clinton, in an act of self-sabotage, illustrated this. During her presidential campaign, Clinton decided to declare that "half of Trump's supporters" belong in what she called a "basket of deplorables", and in case her followers didn't quite latch on, she clarified, "The racist, sexist, homophobic, xenophobic, Islamophobic — you name it." Clinton soon understood that her foolish comment may have cost her a large number of votes and she later expressed regret at letting her misanthropy out. But her comment provides us with a glimpse into the structured, exceptionalist mindset that is at the core of the liberal discourse. We are dealing here with a radical form of exclusiveness and exceptionalism that, unfortunately closely resembles the Jewish secular notion of chosenness.

Systemic and institutional intolerance can be explained in theoretical terms. For an idea to become a 'Jewish religion' it must be defined in terms of a negative dialectic. It must be 'set against something,' or at least be in opposition to something. It must be distinguished or framed by a so-called 'enemy' - the 'reactionary', the 'anti-Semite', the Goy, the 'white' the 'Muslim', the 'rich', the Zionist, the 'anti-Zionist' and so on. For a religion to resemble Judaism it may not need a god but it certainly does need a 'basket of deplorables.' Jewish religions have made an art out of forming ideas and clubs defined by negation which results in religions constantly engaged in struggle with the 'other' - clearly not a template for a peaceful, harmonious existence. In fact, it is a blueprint for relentless paranoia and never ending conflict.

Utopia, Nostalgia, America and the Jew

Utopia, the imaginary ideal, the Eden of collective and universal yearning is at the root of Left and progressive thought. A utopian society is the political and social goal of many leftist and progressive narratives. For others, the perfect society is itself the ideological means toward redemption. Since Left and progressive thought are ruled by the 'ought to be,' no Left or progressive intellectual narrative is impervious to some sort of utopian ideal.

But for more than half of the American people, utopia is nostalgic. The return of the 'American Dream' – the idea of 'being great again' – this is the idyllic vision shared by supporters of both Donald Trump and Bernie Sanders and the Brexit vote in Britain revealed that the Brits are also nostalgic for their nationalist past.

The history of ideas has seen this transition before. Jewish cultural Marxists of the 1930s were shocked by a similar nationalist-patriotic outbreak. Wilhelm Reich and prominent members of the Frankfurt School were bewildered by the widespread popularity of fascism. They couldn't figure out how it was possible that the German and Italian workers favoured 'reactionary' fascism over a 'communist utopia.'

In 1930s Germany as in 2016 America, nostalgia and romanticism invested utopia with meaning – the yearning for a national rootedness over a 'progressive' Shangri La.

The 'Jewish Left' quickly diagnosed what was wrong with the Germans. For Wilhelm Reich it was their repressed sexuality and a few years later, Adorno improved on Reich's paradigm, adding a few other criteria to the model of the authoritarian personality. But Reich and the rest of the cultural Marxists were deluded. Pornography, dildos and the so-called sexual revolution did not mature into a universal emancipation or anything resembling a proletarian revolution. Quite the opposite, they contributed to alienation and suppression of pretty much every precious Western human value.

The Germans and the National Socialists were not sympathetic to Reich and the Frankfurt School, so the latter had to run. The Frankfurt Research Institute relocated at Columbia University in New York City, from where it devoted the next few decades to the political and cultural manipulation of the American people.

Unlike the German fascists who rejected the Jewish, revolutionary, progressive ideologists, it took the American intelligentsia half a century to even start to react to the Institute that had planted identity politics and political correctness at the heart of America's academia, culture, media and politics.

But in 2016 America, the Jewish progressive elite appeared to repeat the same mistake the Frankfurt School and Wilhelm Reich made in the 1930s Germany. The reaction of the likes of Noam Chomsky and the *Jewish Daily Forward* to the American working people was catastrophic and dangerous. Ahead of the election, in a Channel 4 News (UK) interview[69] Chomsky called Trump voters "White poor working class"[70] while the *Forward*[71] called them "White supremacist," "losers" and "bullies."

Just a week before the 2016 presidential election, Jewish academic Cheryl Greenberg referred to Trump as a puppet-master who controls his audience by means of 'dog whistling.' "Trump's references to money, bankers and international conspiracies appear to be deliberate anti-Semitic dog whistles, and his alt-right supporters recognize (and celebrate) that."[72] According to Greenberg, when Trump wants to communicate a message about the Jews, he uses an indecipherable code intelligible only to half of the Americans (and herself).

Greenberg was either optimistic, naive or foolish. Just a few days before the American people made Trump into their next president, she wrote that Trump's popularity is "the

---

69. Noam Chomsky full length interview: Who rules the world now?, Channel 4 News, https://www.youtube.com/watch?v=P2lsEVlqtso

70. As usual it is hard to figure out whether Chomsky is misinformed or just lying. A quick Internet search reveals that Trump's "voters are better off economically compared with most Americans." (The Mythology Of Trump's 'Working Class' Support, Five Thirty Eight, http://fivethirtyeight.com/features/the-mythology-of-trumps-working-class-support/). Trump also enjoys the support of a growing number of educated people (5 myths about Trump supporters, Politico, http://www.politico.com/story/2016/03/5-myths-about-trump-supporters-220158).

71. Donald Trump Hates Losers. Judaism Can't Get Enough of Them, The Jewish Daily Forward, Jay Michaleson 22.8.2016 http://forward.com/opinion/348008/donald-trump-hates-losers-judaism-cant-get-enough-of-them/

72. https://www.washingtonpost.com/posteverything/wp/2016/10/26/donald-trumps-conspiracy-theories-sound-anti-semitic-does-he-even-realize-it/?utm_term=.2ad6832fdfae

final gasping of white supremacy". I thought at the time that Jewish academics expressing such contempt towards half of the American people in the name of a vague, progressive mantra was a very dangerous game.

But what was the real crime of all these 'White losers' and alt-right 'anti-Semites'? Simple, they were nostalgic.

It is clear that Jewish progressive institutions and left icons are horrified by mainstream White folks being nostalgic. Yet, one may wonder why Jewish outlets such as The Forward and Jewish academics such as Greenberg and Chomsky are afraid of other people being nostalgic. After all, Jews are people who are connected to their past and cultural heritage.

The progressive Jew may well grasp that working class nostalgia is for a time when American politics, culture and finance weren't dominated by the likes of Haim Saban[73], George Soros, Goldman Sachs, Noam Chomsky or Sidney Blumenthal; all of whom are totally isolated from production, manufacturing and farming.

The so-called progressives in Democracy Now, Real News, the *Jewish Daily Forward* and the other Soros-funded outlets interpret the 2016 US presidential election as an anti-Jewish tsunami on the verge of a new Holocaust.

But do they have a reason? Has anyone within Trump's coterie even mentioned any intention to harm the Jews, or to curtail Jewish power? Not at all. In fact, the opposite has happened, Trump has regularly sworn allegiance to the Jews

---

73. Haim Saban is an Israeli-American media mogul. He is a major donor to the US Democratic Party and active pro-Israel campaigner in the US.

and their state. And if this is not enough, Trump has a Jewish daughter, has relied heavily on his Jewish son-in-law and, according to Fox News, might as well be "the first Jewish president."[74]

This presents us with a fascinating riddle. The Americans, on the whole, love and support Israel, they may even love America being the alternative Jewish Promised Land. They like the La-la-land fantasy invented by Hollywood and most citizens even like the idea of hard capitalism as dictated by Wall Street. But the progressives at The Forward and the Open Society Institute know very well that the sympathies of the Americans are misplaced. They know that America, like the rest of the West, is a bubble - and it is about to burst.

The Jewish progressive fear of the so-called reactionary and the conservative White is motivated by a profound understanding that the American past was indeed greater than the current progressive-liberal dystopia. They are fearful of a general fatigue of the tyranny of correctness, Identitarian misanthropy and, more than anything else, the lack of a future that is attached to the prominence of Wall Street and Mammonism in general.

So perhaps now we can grasp what seems to be the progressives' excessive aggression towards the so-called White.

If guilt tends to manifest itself through aggression, then

---

74. "Trump is headed to the White House. Did we just elect our first Jewish president?" http://www.foxnews.com/opinion/2016/11/20/trump-is-headed-to-white-house-did-just-elect-our-first-jewish-president.html

to identify Jewish progressive guilt, all we have to do is to work backwards from the aggression to the guilt. In other words, the manifest Jewish progressive aggression towards the White, the Redneck or Trump voters provides a fascinating analytical pathway back towards the core of Jewish guilt.

We also know that guilt often translates into irrational symptoms of anxiety and compulsiveness. Jewish progressives do recognize that the privileged universe in which they operate is inconsistent with the universalist mantra they preach so enthusiastically. But this duplicity, intrinsic to progressive politics, has consequences. It manifests itself via paths of covert aggression.

A close examination of cultural Marxists, Wilhelm Reich, the Frankfurt School and their contemporary progressive followers through a perspective of projected guilt, reveals a devastating picture.

I have come to the conclusion that these intellectual and pseudo-academic narratives within the cultural Marxist milieu, are contrived to blind society to the basic fact that true utopia is nostalgic. They have devoted their lives and careers to the concealment of that which is most obvious and undeniable: that for working people, rootedness is home. The neo-Freudians, neo-Marxists, The Frankfurt School, Wilhelm Reich, the New Left, the critical theorist, the liberal and the progressive – all have one basic mission: to divert attention from the blunders of Mammonism and from those who benefit most from Mammon. This realisation allows us to understand why George Soros, an arch-Mammonite, funds the entire New Left infrastructure through his Open Society Institute. He controls the opposition.

From Goldstein to Soros and Beyond

In his book, *The Invention of the Land of Israel*, Israeli academic Shlomo Sand presents conclusive evidence that the Zionist historical narrative is implausible: the Jewish Exile is a myth, as are the Jewish people and the 'Land of Israel.'

But Sand fails to address the most important question: If Zionism is based on myth, how have the Zionists managed to get away with their lies, and for so long? If the supposed Jewish notion of homecoming and the demand for a Jewish national homeland cannot be historically substantiated, why has it been supported by both Jews and the West for so long? How has the Jewish state managed to celebrate its racist, expansionist ideology at the expense of the Palestinian and Arab people, and for such a long time?

Jewish power is one answer, but what is it? Can this question even be broached without the attendant accusation of anti-Semitism? Can we ever discuss its meaning and scrutinize its politics? Is Jewish power a dark force, managed and manoeuvred by some conspiratorial power? Is it something about which Jews themselves are shy? Quite the opposite: in many cases, Jewish power is celebrated publicly.

"As a proud Jew, I want America to know about our accomplishment. Yes, we control Hollywood," wrote Joel

143

Stein[75] in the *LA Times* in 2008[76] and Stein didn't stop there. He ended his puff piece by stating: "I don't care if Americans think we're running the news media, Hollywood, Wall Street or the government. I just care that we get to keep running them." So how was Joel Stein trying to hide Jewish power?

The American Jewish lobby, AIPAC, is also not reticent about its agenda, its practices or its achievements. AIPAC, CFI in the UK and CRIF in France operate in an overt manner and often brag about their successes.

We have become accustomed to watching our democratically elected leaders queue shamelessly to kneel before their pay-masters. Neocons make no attempt to hide their close Zionist affiliations. Abe Foxman's Anti Defamation League (ADL) had been openly chasing and harassing anyone who dares criticise Israel. And of course, the same applies to the media, banking and Hollywood. Many powerful Jews show no reticence whatsoever when they boast of their bond with Israel, their commitment to Israeli security, Zionist ideology, the primacy of Jewish suffering, Israeli expansionism, and Jewish domination within culture, media, finance, academia and politics.

But, ubiquitous as they are, AIPAC, CFI, ADL etc. are only symptoms of Jewish power. Real Jewish power is actually the power to silence criticism of Jewish power. It is the capacity to determine the boundaries of the political

75. Joel Stein is an American Jewish journalist writing for the Los Angeles Times and is a regular contributor to Time.

76. http://articles.latimes.com/2008/dec/19/opinion/oe-stein19

discourse – and particularly of criticism of itself. Jewish power prevents us from both assessing Jewish power and, more importantly, from discussing its impact.

Popular belief holds that it is 'right wing' Zionists who facilitate Jewish power, but this is woefully inadequate as an explanation. It is actually the 'good', the 'enlightened' and the 'progressive' who ensure that Jewish power is the most effective and forceful power in America and beyond. It is the 'progressives' and 'liberals' who do the most to interfere with our ability to identify the Judeo-centric politics at the heart of neo-conservatism, American imperialism and foreign policy. It is the so-called 'anti' Zionist who effectively blurs our cognisance that Israel is the Jewish state (as it defines itself). After all, if Israel decorates its tanks, flags and bombs with Jewish symbols, should not the rest of us be entitled to ask who are the Jews, what is Judaism, what is Jewishness and how are those three are related?

It was Jewish Left intellectuals who led the charge against Professors John Mearsheimer, Stephen Walt and James Petras' work on the Jewish lobby. It is the so-called 'Jewish progressives' JVP and Max Blumenthal who led the campaign to silence the brilliant Alison Weir and *If Americans Knew*[77]. It is exactly the same herd of progressive Jews who were desperate to silence me, and worked effortlessly to stop the distribution of my previous book

77. *If Americans Knew* is a nonprofit organization that focuses on the Israeli-Palestinian conflict and the foreign policy of the United States regarding the Middle East.

The Wandering Who? Even Occupy AIPAC, the campaign against the most dangerous political lobby in America, is dominated by a few righteous activists who openly identify politically (rather than religiously) as Jews.

We may have to accept that our dissent is not free and, for some time now, we have been manipulated. As George Orwell, already in 1948, somehow managed to see, our opposition is controlled. Emmanuel Goldstein, the pivotal character in Orwell's *1984*, is a Jewish revolutionary, a fictionalised Leon Trotsky. He is the head of a mysterious anti-party organization called The Brotherhood, the author of the most subversive revolutionary text (*The Theory and Practice of Oligarchical Collectivism*), the dissenting voice, the one who speaks truth to power. Orwell understood the use of dissent and in his final novel he exposes Goldstein as merely an invention of Big Brother, a tool that controls the opposition and the boundaries of dissent.

Orwell's personal account of the Spanish Civil War, *Homage to Catalonia*, clearly presaged the creation of Emmanuel Goldstein. It was what Orwell witnessed in Spain that, a decade later, matured into a profound understanding of the use of dissent to control opposition. As I mentioned earlier, my guess is that by the late 1940s, Orwell understood the depth of intolerance as well as the tyrannical and conspiratorial traits at the heart of Big Brother-ish Left politics and praxis.

Our contemporary dissident movement is largely controlled. The list of organisations founded by George Soros' Open Society Institute (OSI) presents a grim picture – pretty much the entire American progressive, liberal and sectarian network is funded by a liberal Zionist billionaire with a dubious ethical record. And like his pro-Zionist counterpart, Haim Saban, Soros does not operate clandestinely. His Open Society Institute provides all the legally required information regarding the vast sums it spends on all its good and important causes.

So one can't accuse Soros or the Open Society Institute of anything sinister such as vetting the political discourse, stifling free speech or even 'controlling the opposition.' All Soros does is support a wide variety of humanitarian causes: human rights, gender equality, gay rights, Democracy Now, democracy later, the Arab 'Spring', the Arab Winter, Black Lives Matter (sometimes), the oppressed, the oppressor, tolerance, intolerance, Palestine, Israel, anti-war, pro-war (when needed), and so on.

Like Orwell's Big Brother that frames dissent by means of controlled opposition, Soros' Open Society Institute sets the boundaries of critical thought. In *1984* it's the Party that invents its own opposition and writes its texts, but within the realm of the post-political era, it is George Soros, the world's arch-Mammonite himself, who enables our own voices of dissent to be heard and we, for our part, react approvingly, willingly and consciously. We learn to compromise our most precious principles to fit the agenda of our paymaster.

The invisible hand metaphor was coined by Adam Smith to describe the self-regulating behaviour of the marketplace. But the visible hand describes a self-regulating reality in which political-fund beneficiaries fully integrate the world-view of their benefactors.

Democracy Now, probably the leading American dissident outlet, has never discussed the Jewish lobby with Professors Mearsheimer, Walt, Petras, Israel Shamir or myself, the leading experts on the topic, who could have informed the American people about how the USA's foreign policy is dominated by the Jewish lobby. Democracy Now opposes the neocon philosophy, but refuses to explore the roots of the neocon's Zio-centric agenda nor would it ever touch the issue of Jewish identity. This media platform may host a Noam Chomsky or a Norman Finkelstein, it may even let Finkelstein chew up Zionist caricature Alan Dershowitz – all very good, but really not good enough.

It is this institutional betrayal, intrinsic to New Left, liberal and progressive politics, that introduced an unbridgeable gulf between American blue-collar workers and the progressive. It is that betrayal that led to the popularity of Donald Trump and Bernie Sanders in the 2016 presidential primaries and it is the attachment between the progressive, the liberal and the Wall Street Mammonites that, in the 2016 election, led Hillary Clinton to a humiliating defeat.

Connecting the Dots

"In theory there is no difference between theory and practice. In practice there is." – **Yogi Berra**

Mammonism vs Production

Western civilization is under the weather. Capitalism as practiced has put us on a path towards global and universal poverty. A total disaster. But capitalism alone does not explain the situation. When America had a prosperous, growing economy and a milkman could support a family of five, it was capitalism that facilitated prosperity. When America was the world's leading manufacturing power, capitalism and the free market drove its economy. The same can be said of Britain, France and other industrial societies. In the West, capitalism provided work for those who wanted to earn a living. But if capitalism was a positive force, why isn't it anymore?

One possible answer is that capitalism is a two-headed beast. One head offers production that is often healthy for society as a whole. The other head is mammon that is trade-orientated: banking, stock market, investment, currency manipulations, etc. Unlike production and manufacturing that engages large numbers of people from many parts of society, mammon is restricted to a tiny fraction. It makes the rich richer but leaves them detached from the rest of society.

Often mammon and manufacturing support each other because production is dependent on investment and financial markets. But not always. While traditional manufacturing involves labour on a large scale, mammon is concerned only with the accumulation of wealth for its own sake and as such, is impervious to social or ethical issues. Care for the worker or for society are foreign to the Mammonite because they have no role in the accumulation of money.

At present, Mammonism is the driving force behind global capitalism and the goal is to maximize wealth accumulation. As a direct result, production and manufacturing must always gravitate to where labour and production are cheapest.

Most Brits are upset by the state of the dystopia in which they live and the Brexit vote indicates that they may think splitting from the European Union will alleviate their problems. They nostalgically crave their pre-Brussels universe. But if Britain's real problem resides in the City of London (London's Wall Street), then fleeing from Brussels is not going to help. The same applies to America. If the core of America's problems spring from Wall Street, neither Trump nor Sanders nor anyone else can save the American people or make America great again - not unless Wall Street's Mammonism becomes a financial instrument dedicated to American manufacturing.

I'd better confess, I offer no original criticism of the dark forces within the capitalist apparatus. These issues were raised almost a century ago by Henry Ford, probably the most innovative industrialist in the history of the

American people.

In his book, *The International Jew* (1920), the eccentric industrialist who voluntarily used company profits to increase workers' wages, pointed to the corrosive impact of Mammonism. Ford insisted that, as opposed to American workers and in total contradiction of the American working ethos, a bunch of speculative capitalists were concerned with one thing only – "wealth for the sake of wealth." According to Ford, the 'international Jew' wasn't interested in production or farming. For Ford, the international Jew sat on Wall Street and speculated on other people's fates, desires, currency, stocks, or shall we say, future.

Ford didn't refer to the Jews as a whole, he didn't criticise the Jews as a race or as an ethnicity. He was aware of the poverty rate within Jewish migrant communities in the USA at the time. He knew also that Jews were not a monolithic group. But Ford did oppose a tiny segment within world Jewry. For him the 'International Jew' was a reference to a bunch of oligarchs and Mammonites. Ford believed that he managed to identify the capitalist trend that was destined to destroy America and Western civilization.

Why did America remain unaffected by this visionary capitalist and his writings?

The Old Testament provides an answer. The Hebrew Bible is a chronicle of shunned prophets. Jewish culture contains a set of strategies designed to suppress visionary and critical voices. The Biblical prophets and their successors are dismissed one after the other: Christ is nailed to the cross, Spinoza was excommunicated and Marxism became a popular Jewish religion just to make sure that the 'revolution' remained in safe hands.

Henry Ford became the anti-Semite *de jour* which was enough to obliterate his dark prophecy. No doubt Ford wasn't suffused with love for the Jews; he may have been a crude Jew hater, but his opposition to the Jewish money-movers was not racial hatred or bigotry towards Jews as a group. As mentioned above, *The International Jew* focuses on only a tiny sector of the Jewish universe; a Jewish elite that by the 1920s was already prominent within American and world finance, banking and investment banking.

Just three days before the 2016 American presidential elections, American Jewish writer Josh Marshal announced to the world that he was upset by the Republican candidate's closing ad. "It›s packed with "anti-Semitic dog whistles, anti-Semitic tropes and anti-Semitic vocabulary."[78] Marshal wrote, echoing Trinity College historian Cheryl Greenberg's analysis.

But what was it that was anti-Semitic about Trump's ad? Marshal answers, "the four readily identifiable American bad guys in the ad are Hillary Clinton, George Soros (financier), Janet Yellen (Federal Reserve Chair) and Lloyd Blankfein (Goldman Sachs CEO)."[79] It's worth mentioning that there was not a single reference in the ad to the ethnicity of any of the above characters. During his campaign, Trump referred to them as corrupted human beings. But it was Josh Marshal who saw them as Jews.

---

78. http://talkingpointsmemo.com/edblog/trump-rolls-out-anti-semitic-closing-ad

79. Ibid

It was actually Josh Marshal who identified Soros, Yellen and Blankfein as 'international Jewish financiers and bankers.'

I don't know whether Trump or Marshal have ever read Ford's International Jew but it seems that, as far as Marshal is concerned, there's no need. Marshal knows exactly who the Mammonites are – he just insists the rest of us avoid the topic. But the truth cannot be denied. The international bankers and financiers who brought America and the world to its knees are no abstract category. They are people with faces and names. I guess that in 2016 America, pointing at Wall Street leaders is much the same as burning a synagogue.

Genius, Devious or both?

"The brief legal emancipation of Jews during the Napoleonic wars released unparalleled economic, professional, and cultural energies. It was though a high dam had suddenly been breached." – Amos Elon[80]

In 1982, Israeli political commentator Oded Yinon published an Israeli Strategic Plan for the Middle East[81]. He predicted that a growing number of communities in the Middle East and the Muslim world would drift away from the so-called Western ethos and its vision of 'enlightenment.' According to Yinon, Israel could counter this development

80. *The Pity of It All - A portrait of the German-Jewish Epoch, 1743 -1933* (New York: Picador, 2002) pg 6

81. http://www.globalresearch.ca/greater-israel-the-zionist-plan-for-the-middle-east/5324815

through a simple plan: ensure that the Arabs would be consumed by internal conflicts and sectarian wars, i.e., that Sunnis, Shias, Alawites, Kurds and Arab Christians killing each other would be good for Israel.[82] By the time the Syrian war had become a humanitarian disaster, it became clear that the Israeli analyst was proved to be rather farsighted.

How is it possible that an obscure Israeli managed to produce such an accurate forecast? Was Oded Yinon a genius or did he possess a devious mind? And what about Wilhelm Reich, Freud, Marx, Adorno, Marcuse, Edward Bernays and Norman Lear? Were they extremely smart or just extremely manipulative? In the last part of this book, I will delve into some analytical models that help explain what sustains the current Jewish ideological and cultural hegemony in the West. Like Yuri Slezkine, I believe that Jews have become the premiere symbol and standard of modern life everywhere. Jews have become a dominant element in Western society. But the question is, why?

In recent years there has been extensive discussion about the notion of 'Jewish genius' as demonstrated by facts such as that Jews are highly overrepresented amongst the list of Nobel laureates. Of course, gaining the Nobel Prize isn't in itself an infallible indication of innovative thought. Nobel laureateship may just be a prestigious club managed by

---

82. It is important to mention that the Israeli intelligence elite is not united in its view of the Arab Spring and Arab Sectarian wars. Some of the Israel's security experts have been insisting all along that the Arab spring can potentially destabilise the region and eventually introduce some dangerous hostile and unpredictable new elements.

political and tribal considerations. Still, it is hard to ignore that some incredibly clever and powerful Jews are very visible within Western culture, finance, science and media. But does that necessarily mean that there is a special cognitive ability unique to the Jews? Are they really smarter than other people? Not at all.

Let us examine the prominence of Jews in our society and attempt to untangle the sociology and culture that drives Jewish influence in political lobbying, academia, culture, media and finance.

Ashbachat ha-geza – Refining the Race

Ashbachat ha-geza refers, in Hebrew, to the active process of refining and perfecting the self-proclaimed Jewish race.

For several hundred years, some suggest as many as 1500 years, European Jews practiced a unique form of matchmaking. In the Jewish ghetto and *shtetl*[83], the rich Jew (*gvir*), usually a merchant or a moneylender, married his daughter (*bat ha-gvir*) to the Talmudic protégée, the young rabbinical student destined to become a leading Talmudic scholar (*iloui ba-torah*). Jewish folklore is saturated with tales exploring these cultural manoeuvrings.

From a Jewish perspective, the procedure was effective. Jews were living in isolated ghettos and *shtetls*, detached from their surrounding social environments. They created a cultural and social system that maintained an elite, well

---

83. *Shtetl* – Yiddish, a small Jewish town or village in eastern Europe.

versed in religious texts and the tribal ethos, but also adept at handling material affairs. They basically made sure that the right people would be available for the top positions. In practical terms, their society subscribed to a form of an educated meritocracy.

Whether intentionally or not, this practice contributed to the emergence of a tiny, European, Jewish cognitive elite that was equally sophisticated in both Torah and in finance. Since, at the time, Jews and gentiles were almost always separated by walls that limited interaction, the members of the Jewish cognitive elite were unlikely to measure their skills in comparison to the gentile population.

At the same time as Jews were nurturing their best and brightest, European gentiles were doing the opposite. When Catholic institutions spotted a particularly smart boy, they sent him to the monastery where vows of celibacy would ensure that his intelligence would die with him.

The Return of the Bell Curve

The bell curve is a popular diagram that depicts how different qualities are distributed in nature. It has also been utilized to show distribution of cognitive ability within any given society or community.

In figure A[84], the horizontal axis represents cognitive ability and, as we move from the left to the right, ability

---

84 The bell curve diagrams in this book should be seen as abstract visual aids rather than scientific or statistic representations.

increases. The vertical height of the diagram shows the number of people at a given ability, the number increasing as the line goes up. As you can see in figure A, on the left side of the diagram we detect a small number of people with lower cognitive ability (1), as we move to the right we notice a big increase of people with average cognitive ability (2) as we move further to the right, the number decreases as we see a smaller number of highly-abled people. (3).

Figure A

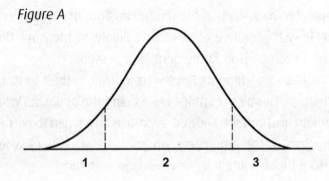

In a normal, traditional, European society, the elite or aristocracy would look more or less like a squashed bell curve.

Figure B

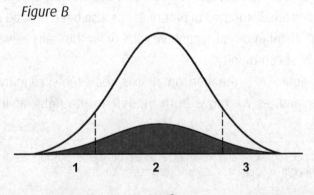

In the diagram above (figure B), the grey area shows ability distribution within traditional European aristocracy in comparison with the rest of the society (the upper curve). Noticeably, European aristocracy wasn't a cognitive class because membership in the aristocracy was determined by lineage rather than by ability. Aristocracy passed to the oldest rather than the most able son. Consequently, a few of Europe's aristocrats have been somewhat limited in cognitive terms (1). Many more aristocrats were average in terms of their abilities (2) and just a few are especially clever (3). As you can see, the distribution of cognitive ability within European aristocracy was similar to the distribution of ability in the rest of society.

The Brits tinkered with the system of the European aristocracy. They grasped that leading a nation with imperial inclinations may require a strong cognitive elite. Like the rabbinical Jews, the British Empire invested in the cognitive abilities of the ruling elite and, by means of the peerage system, invited able subjects within the military, academia, civil services, clergy and arts to join its upper classes.

Figure C

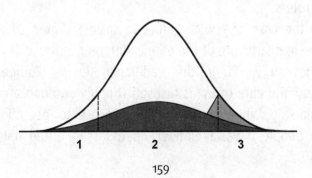

159

In figure C, you can notice a little (light) grey bump in the range of high cognitive ability (3). This little light grey area represents an injection of highly able people into the British ruling class. But unlike the European Jewish traditional society that specialized in money and scholarship, the Brits welcomed ability in varied and diverse forms, and that in turn contributed enormously to the sufficiency of the empire. This unique British exercise also supported the emergence of a relatively liberal and tolerant intellectual attitude among the British elite. This may be the foundation of British academic openness, diversity and debating culture.

Interestingly, as I write, the current British Prime Minister, Theresa May, is campaigning to reintroduce grammar schools (state funded, highly selective academically orientated secondary schools) into the British education system. May believes that for Britain to prevail, it must recruit the most able people of all classes and train them to lead their society.

The British Empire wasn't alone in searching for gifted people to join the elite. The Ottoman Empire also sought its most talented and gifted subjects, and made them into rulers.

In the case of Jewish European society (figure D) the shape and structure of the elite is different to those of the non-Jewish world. In the traditional, Jewish, European society, the elite (grey) is focused strongly on finance and scholarship. While the traditional Jewish elite rose above other people, it was a relatively open class for gifted males.

The Jewish society invested in education and searched for young Talmudic talents in the Jewish ghettos and even in some of the remote shtetls.

Figure D

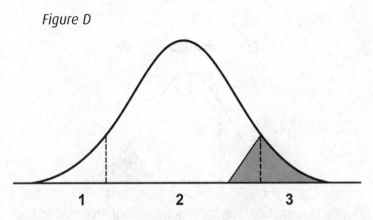

But the investment by traditional Jewish society in building an elite with high cognitive ability had a downside. By aggressively building a cognitive elite, the Jewish leadership removed from the Jewish masses the most gifted males. Through the rabbinical educational institutions, Jewish society constantly monitored the extended community to search for potential rabbinical talents. Since the elite class was open, once a protégé was identified, he would be lifted out of the larger community and sent to a prominent yeshiva, usually in Western Europe.

In the European Jewish world, cognitive partitioning had geographic effects that resulted in a geographic cognitive divide between East and West (Figure E). The lower cognitive class was largely centred on Western Russia in the Pale of Settlement[85], while the more able Jews were sent to Jewish centres further west, in such European conurbations as Prague, Moravia and Frankfurt.

Figure E

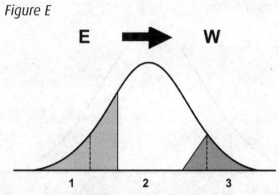

In practice an East/West geographic cognitive divide was created between the rabbinical and financial elite that was centred in Ashkenaz – the Germanic countries and central Europe – and 'The Yiddish Nation,' as Shlomo Sand labels the Jews of the East (*Ostjuden*) who were largely considered lower class.[86]

Within the traditional Jewish class division, Eastern Jews were regarded as suited only for manual labour. In Hebrew and Yiddish literature, they are occasionally referred to as hewers of wood (*hotvei etzim*), and drawers of water (*shoavei maim*).

---

85. Pale of Settlement was a western region of Imperial Russia, where Jews were allowed to reside permanently.

86. It is worth mentioning that the East/West cognitive divide wasn't exactly an iron rule. There were a few vibrant rabbinical and cultural centers in various East European cities such as Vilnius, Krakow, Odessa and Warsaw.

The Jewish authors Shai Agnon and Shalom Aleichem were fascinated by these Yiddish communities of the Pale. Aleichem's *Fiddler on The Roof* explores this divide. The famous song from Fiddler, entitled *If I Were a Rich Man*, was originally titled in Yiddish *If I Were a Rothschild*. The lyrics delve into the longings of the *Ostjuden*, represented by Tevye, the milkman, and explore the sharp class divide within European Jewry. It is possible that the 19th century Eastern-European Jewish affinity to Marxism, and later to Bolshevism, had something to do with this internal (cognitive) Jewish class divide.

Emancipation

The French revolution and the spirit of enlightenment greatly changed the traditional Jewish community. After the revolution, France and a growing number of European nations invited the Jews to join their society as equal citizens. This shift in the European treatment of Jews is known as The Jewish Emancipation. Within a decade or two, Jews associated with the cognitive elite had managed to assimilate and become themselves a leading and dominant European class.

These gifted Jews claimed significant roles within academia, the arts, medical schools and law departments. They entered governments and politics and before long they were involved with their new nations' national and global affairs. Probably the House of Rothschild is the most prominent example of that spectacular social phenomenon.

But the Rothschilds weren't alone. The Warburg Family[87], the Bischoffsheim and the Speyer families also prospered. And banking was just part of the story because the Marxist resistance to banking, mammon and capitalism was also dominated by members of the same cognitive class – perhaps they hated in themselves such an affinity to Mammon.

In the years following the emancipation, the Jewish intelligentsia were incredibly successful. Jewish elites were uniquely suited to succeed in both mammon and scholarship – not only were they often more sophisticated in certain fields, they were also far more clannishly organized than their European elite counterparts.

Marketing and Strategy

This is awkward and uncomfortable territory. The above reading of Jewish, European, rabbinical society suggests that, for generations, some segments within world Jewry engaged in a eugenic and meritocratic exercise. However, what we have learned so far confirms that the Jewish European traditional elite was somehow different from other elites.

It must again be emphasized that the reference to Jewish high achievers applies to an isolated, tiny class within the European Jewish world. It doesn't refer to the Jews as a

---

87. Paul Moritz Warburg (1868 – 1932) was a Jewish German-born American banker, and an early advocate of the U.S. Federal Reserve System.

whole or Jews as a so-called race, people or ethnicity, and it also defies the popular misleading notion of the Jewish genius. Instead of the Jews as innately clever, here we are focused on a particular, and quite specialized ability, spread within a tiny meritocratic sector situated at the hub of the European Jewish world.

Those who enrol in a university often encounter amongst their professors the common mismatch between impressive academic abilities and their complete inadequacy in other areas. In spite of great abilities in maths, physics or philosophy, some of our scholars are totally useless at everything else – and this includes the marketing of their ideas and the promotion of their writings.

But when it comes to Jewish intellectuals, we often find the opposite. Jewish academics aren't just good at scholarship, they are often also highly effective in marketing their thoughts and even transforming them into new grand theories. Marx was very good at marketing himself, certainly better than Engels. Freud, some would argue, was far less interesting than Jung or Lacan but, somehow, together with his global network of disciples, he managed to implant some pretty disturbing ideas into our popular culture and to alter the way in which we perceive ourselves. Wilhelm Reich managed to shove Americans into wooden boxes while collecting royalties for the sex revolution. While Gramsci, probably the most advanced socialist revolutionary and the ideological father of cultural Marxism, died in a prison cell, his followers within the Frankfurt School added a student revolution to their résumés. Similarly, Norman Lear made us into 'Meatheads' and Edward Bernays reduced us to consumers.

One may speculate on the intellectual legacy of some of our most vocal Jewish intellectuals in, let's say, one hundred years. What will remain of Noam Chomsky, Bernard-Henri Lévy, Alan Dershowitz, Theodor Adorno or Emmanuel Levinas? My guess is not a lot. Yet, these Jewish thinkers have been incredibly successful in promoting their ideas on a global scale while also advocating different aspects of Jewish national interests.

The Role of Jewish Humour

We have delved into the stratum of the Jewish cognitive elite, but what about the Jewish underclass? What about the Yiddish Nation, those hewers of wood and drawers of water, the *Ostjuden* left behind in the Pale of Settlement?

Jewish humour, better described by Shlomo Sand as Yiddish humour, was definitely a Yiddish, underclass enterprise. Sand went on to note that Albert Einstein or Spinoza did not spend much time cracking jokes about their wider community in Yiddish. So what we regard as Jewish humour, is largely a Yiddish, *folkish* cult, the means by which the *Ostjuden* in the East dealt with their ordeal. It was also one way of resolving the Jewish class division by helping the underclasses to identify with the elite.

Most 19th century Yiddish jokes centre on a narrative in which the ordinary Jew outsmarts the *dummkopf* Goy. There are endless variations on this somewhat racially-orientated theme but always it is the Jew who wins out, leaving the poor, befuddled Goy confused by his own gullibility.

Of course the reality was somewhat different. It was not the Goy who was left behind but the *Ostjuden*, surrounded by ghetto walls and oppressed by a hostile environment, moulded by their Christian rulers and sometimes also by their own Jewish elite. Nineteenth century Yiddish humour allowed the Yiddish-speaking Eastern Jew to identify with the Western Ashkenazi cognitive elite and look down at the local gentile oppressor. Through a joke, the Eastern Jew could elevate himself to the rank of a Rothschild or a Warburg.

Here are two such jokes.

In a city in Poland there were two beggars, working the entrance to the railway station every Sunday. One was a bearded, orthodox Jew, ragged and unpleasant looking, the other was a tidy, clean-shaven Christian with a white shirt and a shining crucifix hanging from his neck. As one would expect, the Christian beggar collected a lot of money, while the Jew was left standing, poor, humiliated and often abused. The anti-Semites cursed him and spat on him and he rarely managed to collect a single penny.

After a few weeks, a Catholic priest, obviously a humble humanist, approached the Jew and politely told him, "My dear son, it hurts me to see members of my church treating you as badly as they do but coming to our city every Sunday may not be such a wise move. It's clear you don't manage to make a single penny, but look at this Christian fellow next to you, look how well he is doing. I would kindly advise you to go back to your ghetto.

The Jewish beggar, smiled to himself, turns to the Christian beggar next to him, and, in Yiddish, says: "Oi Moishe, this *shlemazl*[88] Goy thinks he can teach us about marketing?"

The joke is pretty straightforward – these stupid Goyim, they just don't understand how smart we Jews are. Always, we're one step ahead. Unfortunately, the reality was quite different. The Jews in the East at that time led a dismal existence, they were oppressed, harassed and heavily discriminated against. Jokes like this were a part of their Jewish identification, the means by which the oppressed could express their tribal affinity to the able, the shrewd, the rulers of the world.

Here is another Jewish joke; dark and offensive, it is as rude as it is funny:

There's a pogrom. A bunch of drunken, Ukrainian Cossacks enter the shtetl. First they kill the men, then they kill the teenage boys, then they drink all the vodka and before long, they start to rape the women. Finally, when their sexual thirst is sated, they start to search for gold. But before they find any gold, they find in an attic, an old grandma. Postponing their search for gold, the Cossacks strip off their clothes and prepare for another sexual assault. When the mother and the daughters downstairs realize that their 95-year old grandma is about

---

88. Shlemazl - (Yiddish) hopeless, clumsy and naive character.

to be raped, they are distraught. In desperation, they shout up the stairs:

"Oi vey. Mercy, mercy! Leave her alone! We'll give you all the gold you want."

But up in her attic, Grandma has a different plan:

"What do you mean, 'leave her alone?' A pogrom is a pogrom!"

So again, from a Jewish point of view, even an old grandma has more sophistication than those bestial, Cossack, yobs.

Jewish humour is always political, in that it always conveys a message[89] and this Yiddish humour allowed the Jewish, Eastern lower classes to transcend their existential burden. In their jokes they could identify with the Western, Jewish, cognitive elite and remove from their hearts and minds the huge distance between the gifted and the retarded, between Tevye the Milkman and Baron de Rothschild.

---

89. It may be important to mention that 20th century American Jewish humor conveys the opposite message. Woody Allen is mocking the 'stereotypical clumsy dysfunctional Jew'. Larry David's Curb Your Enthusiasm television comedy also ridicules the self-centred hedonist character. Mel Brooks exaggerates the Jewish symptoms ad absurdum and Sarah Silverman wants to kill Christ again. These Jewish comedians made self-deprecation into an art form. While sarcastically mocking Jewish stereotypes, they disarm any opposition or criticism of Jewish dominance and political power. By openly owning what some would regard as problematic Jewish symptoms, these Jewish entertainers manage, by means of humour, to dismantle the dissent to the Jew. While the so-called anti-Semite accuses the Jew of being a hedonistic, self-centred, capitalist, usurious, Christ killer, David, Allen, Silverman and Brooks' answer is simply, 'Okay, now tell us something we don't know.'

The Clever of Zion

The delicate relationship between the Jewish cognitive elite and the Jewish lower classes may also be a key to understanding the success of Zionism.

In 2004, the Israeli *Haaretz* newspaper revealed that eugenics was an established narrative amongst early Zionists. In an article titled *To Maintain the Purity of Our Race, Degenerate Jews Must Avoid Giving Birth*,[90] the Israeli outlet confessed that "eugenics was not seen as a 'bad idea' in the early days of Zionism." According to the paper, key figures within the Zionist establishment offered to castrate the mentally ill, encourage reproduction among the intelligentsia, reduce the birth-rate in Eastern Jewish communities (Arab Jews), and ensure, as much as possible, that only a healthy and fit baby saw the light of day.

One of the most prominent eugenicists in Mandate Palestine was the leading Zionist medical authority Dr. Yosef Meir[91]. In 1934 Meir wrote "for us, eugenics in general, and the prevention of the transmission of hereditary disorders in particular, is even greater importance than for all other nations!"

In the early fifties Dr. Meir published an article which criticised the 'reproduction cash prize' PM Ben-Gurion

---

90. http://www.haaretz.co.il/misc/1.1558449 (Hebrew only)

91. Dr. Yosef Meir acquired his education in Vienna, he served for thirty years as the head of the biggest health service provider in Palestine and later Israel (Kupat Cholim Klalit). Meir Hospital in Kfar Saba is named after him.

promised each woman who gave birth to ten children: "We have no interest in the tenth child or even the seventh child of families of Eastern origin (Arab Jews)... In reality today there are often prayers for a second child in the family that belong to the intelligentsia."

Cognitive partitioning, eugenics and biologism were deeply rooted in early Zionist thinking. According to *Haaretz*, Dr. Max Nordau, who was second to Herzl in the early days of Zionism, and Dr. Arthur Ruppin, the head of the Israeli office of the World Zionist Organisation, both believed that eugenics must be at the "forefront of Jewish national renewal movement and settlement."

However, these supremacist ideological elements were institutionally suppressed in the 1950s for two reasons.

First, the young Israel was dependent on the mass immigration of Arab Jews for cheaper but still Jewish labour. Instead of an internal Jewish West/East divide, the new Hebrews were united against the new 'enemy', the Arabs in general and the Palestinians in particular. Accordingly, Israel, at least ideologically and theoretically, bridged the cognitive divide. Many would rightly argue that, on the contrary, Israel is racially divided between Ashkenazi and Arab Jews. Moreover, statistics suggest that the cognitive and social divide in Israel is amongst the widest in the West.

Second, following the Holocaust, Zionists and Israeli institutions felt compelled to conceal the similarities between Zionist supremacy (as explored by Meir, Nordau, Rupin and others) and Hiltlerian thinking.

The truth of the matter is that Zionism wasn't very popular

amongst the Jewish masses in the beginning of the 20th century – and it wasn't that popular in the 1930s either, nor even by 1948 when, after years of trying, there were still only 600,000 Jews in Palestine. Then in 1967, all of a sudden, Zionism pretty much became the voice of the Jews.

But is it really a surprise that Zionism became so popular amongst Jews? Look at what the Zionists achieved. They almost entirely ethnically-cleansed the indigenous people of the land, dismissed all international condemnations and a large number of UN resolutions, sent the Western super powers to fight bloody war after bloody war on their behalf, and they continue to keep an entire region in a constant state of nuclear alert. And best of all, they have got away with it!

But is this because the Jews are so clever? Is it because they constitute a unique race or ethnicity? Although the Jewish state poses a serious threat to world peace, for Jews, Zionism and Israel's success is seriously impressive and many Jews believe that Israel proves that there are indeed unique Jewish racial qualities. But Jews may not be as clever as they think and, by the way, they are certainly not a race, nor even an ethnicity. But still, they have managed to form a significantly able elite and, in spite of the secularization and assimilation, have managed to maintain and promote a tribal, clannish culture that continues to be celebrated all over the world.

American historian Norman Finkelstein recently concluded that American Jews are drifting away from Zionism and their support of Israel is dwindling. Whether Finkelstein is correct or not, it is important to understand that it doesn't really matter what the Jews (masses or individuals) think about Zionism or Israel. The Jewish world is not a democratic apparatus, nor does it claim to be. In the Jewish universe, led by the Jewish cognitive elite, it is mammon that sets the tone. All that matters is where billionaire investors George Soros, Haim Saban and Sheldon Adelson put their money.

These oligarchs have an impact that far exceeds the fate of the Jewish state or even of the Jewish people – they, and others like them, truly shape the American universe.

Ten days before the 2016 election, when it seemed that a Clinton victory was certain, the *Jewish Daily Forward* actually bragged about the fact that "the top five Donors to the Hillary Clinton campaign are all Jewish,"[92] At the time, it looked as if once again, the Jewish billionaires had got it right. In fact, a month-and-a-half before the election, the same publication reported that "Jewish donors shun Donald Trump — 95% of contributions go to Hillary Clinton."[93] It won't surprise you then, to find out that, on November 9th, when it became clear that it was actually Donald Trump who had won the election, the *Forward* was quick to change its tune. "7 big-Bucks Jewish Donors Like Sheldon Adelson Lead

92. http://forward.com/news/352719/top-5-donors-to-hillary-clinton-campaign-are-all-jewish/ The Forward provides the names and briefly states their credentials: Donald Sussman, a hedge fund manager; J.B. Pritzker, a venture capitalist, Haim Saban, the Israeli-American entertainment mogul, George Soros, hedge funder and Daniel Abraham founder of SlimFast

93. http://forward.com/news/breaking-news/350531/jewish-donors-shun-donald-trump-95-of-contributions-go-to-hillary-clinton/

Trump Inauguration Committee"[94] was the headline some eight days later, and the *Forward* also reported that, "nine out of the twenty names listed on the [Donald Trump] transition team's announcement released Monday are Jewish. Several of them are on the Republican Jewish Coalition board."[95]

Despite the fact that Trump received only 5% of Jewish donors' money, according to the *Forward*, nearly 50% of his transition team were Jewish[96]. I guess that Trump's top Jewish donor, the casino magnate Sheldon Adelson, can teach George Soros and Haim Saban a thing or two about presidential gambling. Or perhaps not. When it comes to presidential elections, nothing beats putting your bucks on both candidates – which, in effect, is exactly what Saban, Soros and Adelson did.

By now, we are beginning to grasp where the Jewish oligarchy stands on American political affairs, but where does this leave the American people?

The End of The Empire

In the pre-WWII capitalist west, cognitive abilities were distributed throughout society. In early 20th century

---

94. http://forward.com/news/breaking-news/354741/7-big-bucks-jewish-donors-like-sheldon-adelson-lead-trump-inauguration-comm/

95. Ibid

96. "Nine out of the 20 names listed on the transition team's announcement released Monday are Jewish." http://forward.com/news/breaking-news/354741/7-big-bucks-jewish-donors-like-sheldon-adelson-lead-trump-inauguration-comm/

America, there was an expanding economy, dedicated to manufacturing and productivity, where able and gifted people mixed daily with the slightly less gifted. In many cases, they worked side-by-side on the never-ending assembly lines. Manufacturing raised the demand for manual labour and cognitive ability was often not the most important labour skill.

Since the 1970s, America and the West have gone through a radical transition. The rapid technological evolution in automation, robotics and computers has led to an ongoing decrease in the need for manual labour. Our love affair with free and globalized markets, international trade deals and the service economy made the situation of working people even worse. Most western industries were obliterated, while at the same time there has been a fairly constant demand for workers in high ability professions (programmers, engineering, sciences, marketing analysts and so on). And if this combination was not enough to impoverish the working people, we also see the emergence of new barriers between the new cognitive elite and the rest of society.

In line with these developments, the western worker has been reduced to a mere consumer. Those who consume and maintain a reasonable credit rating are respected citizens while others, who were until recently a working class but now are a workless class, are gradually ejected from the game. Pushed into segregated quarters, known by sociologists as the underclass, their fate is basically sealed.

This bleak picture describes the story of the declining of Detroit, Oakland, Baltimore, Newark, and also Liverpool and

Paris. More and more, we see cities segregated by acquisition and attainment – but the barriers are not only socio-economic but also strongly correlated with certain abilities.

In the early 1990s, in their book, *The Bell Curve*, Richard J. Herrnstein and Charles Murray predicted this growing divide. They envisaged a catastrophic, growing gulf between the able and the less able. They could see the emergence of cognitive partitioning and they warned the American people that their society was speeding toward a disaster. Murray and Herrnstein's warnings were met with a wall of resentment and even abuse led by progressive, popular scientist Stephen J. Gould who incidentally, soon after his death, was exposed as a fraud[97].

Figure F

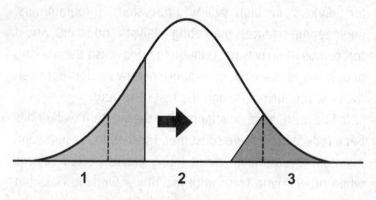

---

97 Soon after his death, it became apparent that Gould was an academic fraudster who fabricated and misrepresented the work of Samuel George Morton. To read more: Fraud in the Imputation of Fraud, Robert Trivers Ph.D. https://www.psychologytoday.com/blog/the-folly-fools/201210/fraud-in-the-imputation-fraud

Figure F will help us to understand the current state of cognitive partitioning within Western, post-industrial society and in America in particular. The dark grey area (3) represents the able as well as the gifted. The light grey area (1 and part of 2) represents the underclass – those who are less gifted and are left behind. The black arrow to the right points at the disastrous fact that this sector is constantly growing because even as the demand for manual labour drops, the underclass expands.

More and more people are losing the means necessary to sustain consumption and are sentenced to deprivation. Sooner or later they will be relegated to the underclass. Their supposed offence is simple: they are not gifted enough to survive the current world order. A century ago, it was perhaps only those who could not understand instructions who were unable to work. Today, people with average and even high mental ability may struggle to support themselves and their families.

But here is an observation I find fascinating. The cognitive partitioning that is now apparent within almost every Western society, is basically an exact replica of the partitioning we observed earlier within Jewish traditional society. Just as in traditional Jewish society, in society as a whole we now experience a complete (geographical, socio-economic and cultural) segregation between the abled and those who are just left behind.

Is it a coincidence that the cognitive partitioning that today divides America is identical with that which divided European Jewish traditional society two hundred years ago? It depends who you ask.

The progressive answer would most likely be that the similarity between the two social settings is by chance, and it would be a wrong to draw any rational conclusions from a simple coincidence. But if you asked Henry Ford, the man who, as early as 1920, detected that dangerous path in American capitalism, you would discover that America was destined to fall into that very trap. Regardless of any technological developments or any shift towards global markets, America was heading towards cognitive partitioning and, in this connection, it was impossible to ignore the vast over-representation, within American finance, culture and media, of what he, Henry Ford, termed the 'International Jews.' For Ford, it was the socially remote, fiscally parasitic Wall Street financier, who was and still is a constant threat to the American ethos of productivity.

The truth may be somewhere in the middle. The decrease in demand for manual labour has been the direct outcome of technological developments (robotics, automation, computers etc.) that have nothing to do with Ford's 'International Jew.' Yet, it is hard to overlook the obvious, that the Jewish elite is a forceful element within the American ruling classes. This is in part because some Jews are indeed very gifted, but it is also because European Jews have for so long been operating within a cognitively partitioned society that, for Jews, such a society just feels like home.

This is a crucial point. Jews are not the only ethnic group over-represented within the American elite but they are probably the most dominant politically and culturally within

American culture, far more so than, for instance, Koreans. And why? Because, unlike Koreans or anyone else, the condition of cognitive partitioning is deeply rooted in their culture.

Edward Bernays' notion of the 'invisible government' points to this partition between the able and the masses. By 1928, it was clear to Bernays that for democracy to sustain itself, the gifted must be able to manipulate the masses' desires and needs by means of propaganda. For Bernays, cognitive partitioning was an elementary ingredient of democratic existence.

On the other hand, the inability to notice cognitive partitioning may explain why the people who claimed to be 'the ninety-nine per cent' have never managed to draw even 1% onto the streets. The slogan "We are the 99%," might have led the Occupy Wall Street Movement[98] onto the streets but it didn't lead to social change – and we can easily grasp why. The term 'ninety-nine per cent' was inherently misleading. It pointed at a socioeconomic divide between 'us' (the people) and 'them', (the 'filthy rich').

But the 99% vs the 1% is not just a socioeconomic division, it may as well be a cognitive partition (1% being the cognitive elite) which the Left, the New Left, the progressives and the liberals desperately try to conceal. And why do they wish to hide this reality? Probably because Left-leaning ideologies

---

98 Occupy Wall Street (OWS) is the name given to a protest movement that began on September 17, 2011 in the Wall Street financial district, receiving global attention and spawning the Occupy movement against social and economic inequality worldwide.

do not possess the theoretical and ideological means to deal with biology. For biology does not sit well with the ideas of equality, social change, the dream of what ought to be. For the Left, biology is a journey's end.

So is it possible that the attempt to break society by means of ID politics also helps hide the fact that, for all our social-justice sophistication, our society is subject to crude cognitive segregation? Perhaps this is why Soros's Open Society Institute invests so heavily in sectarian and Identitarian politics. From a Mammonite perspective, race and gender wars feel much safer than a communist revolution. After all, in a race war, it is the oppressed who often kill each other instead of chasing their true oppressors within the oligarchy and capital's' financial quarters.

Sometimes I wonder if Professor Herrnstein, the phenomenally clever Harvard professor and the co-author of *The Bell Curve*, was the first to detect the emerging partitioning of American society only because partitioning was imbued in his Jewish upbringing. I suspect that Herrnstein realized that America was becoming a mirror image of the European Jewish ghetto.

The New Left hated *The Bell Curve*. Progressives and liberals portrayed the book as a crude racist text. But the book was a rarity in the social sciences, a meticulously researched and documented, scientific but also prophetic text which accurately predicted the destruction of American working people, both middle and lower classes. It envisaged ghettoized cities split by a cognitive divide.

But just as Herrnstein might have gleaned some insight

from his Jewish heritage, I also wonder whether Stephen J Gould, who led the attack on *The Bell Curve* was also motivated by some tribal interests? Did he attempt to conceal the depth of the emerging 'Jewification' of the American social order?

At the end of the day, Gould won and America and Americans were left to their fate. But an ethical society should care for all of its members, that they live and thrive regardless of their cognitive ability. Perhaps if we listened to Herenstein and examined his argument, we could rescue tens of millions of Americans from poverty and depravation.

An Anecdote

The Bell Curve and its authors were attacked on many fronts but for our purposes, two are especially notable. First, they were criticized for being unscientific in their use of IQ tests to determine cognitive ability. Second, they made comparisons among different populations and races, leading to accusations of racism and biological determinism.

Opposition to IQ tests is not new. Critics of IQ measurement insist that the tests don't really measure intelligence or ability but really only measure the ability to score well on IQ tests. I tend to agree with this position so, when discussing this book I have avoided counting or even mentioning IQ or any other particular measurement of intelligence. Ability is both vague and concrete: like love, you may not be able to describe it but you know it when you see it. I don't know John Coltrane's IQ score, but I know he was one of the most inspiring and gifted men ever. Similarly, I don't know Barack Obama's IQ score but I can see that his cognitive ability is far above average. But it isn't just Coltrane and Obama who are noticeably able. It is more than likely that Hilary Clinton would score a higher IQ result than Donald Trump, yet when it came to becoming a president, Trump proved superior in his 'ability' to *get* himself elected. Ability, so it seems, is determined by a myriad of qualities, many of them are impossible to quantify or measure. So, when discussing ability, I refer to it without reference to how that ability is determined.[99]

But the IQ debate about this best-seller was nothing compared to the storm Herrnstein and Murray faced for making comparisons among populations and races.

Herrnstein and Murray argued that if the bell curve A (Figure G) represents the distribution of IQ within the white American population and B represents the IQ distribution within the Ashkenazi Jewish and Asian American communities, then according to Herrnstein and Murray, the average IQ of Jews and Asian-Americans is slightly higher than the average of White Americans. This assertion, that Ashkenazi Jews and Asians were slightly cleverer than their 'White' American neighbours caused no controversy.

---

99. It is crucial to mention that Herrnstein and Murray addressed their critics and insisted that IQ measured cognitive adaptability. As such, a person who scores 180 IQ in Manhattan may struggle to achieve even an average IQ in Kabul.

Figure G

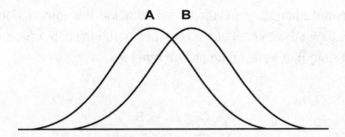

But when Herrnstein and Murray argued that the average IQ score of the Black population C (Figure H) was lower than it was for White Americans, as you can guess, all hell broke loose. In the eyes of American media, academia and beyond, the two researchers were transformed into racist bigots.

Figure H

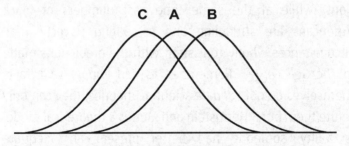

I am not able to properly assess the accuracy of Herrnstein and Murray's findings but, as a jazz musician, dedicated to African-American music and enthralled by the genius of Miles Davis, Monk, John Coltrane, Duke Ellington, Charlie Parker, and the rest I can see what outraged so many people about The Bell Curve.

Yet, there is a crucial problem we must address.

If we look at the comparisons Herrnstein and Murray made amongst populations and combine this information with what we know about cognitive partitioning in America (Figure I), a devastating picture emerges.

Figure I

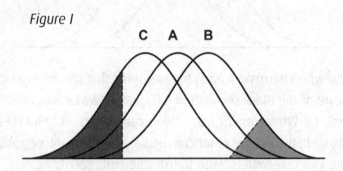

Ashkenazi Jews and Asian Americans are vastly overrepresented within the American elite (light grey on the right) while at the same time vast numbers of black Americans are struggling and combating poverty – all circumstances wholly consistent with the predictions made in *The Bell Curve*. Remember, as Karl Popper said, facts themselves do not *validate* scientific theories, they can only refute them but if Herrnstein and Murray's theoretical model is faulty, someone had better present an adequate alternative.

In the 1970s Herrnstein predicted a cultural and demographic separation between the very intelligent and the rest of us. We can, for correctness' sake, continue to avoid the topic, as we have done for the last five decades.

We can concur with segregation and, as we have been doing, allow the weak to be obliterated. Or we can confront the problem and accept that society must build the instruments and institutions to support all people regardless of their cognitive ability. Such tools will most likely involve productivity, manufacturing, and agriculture here at home - all things that the smart boys in Wall Street and the City of London prefer to buy more cheaply elsewhere.

It is no surprise that the Left, the New Left, the liberals and the progressives didn't welcome *The Bell Curve*. The reality of cognitive partitioning defies the fantasy of the 'ought to be' and the utopian dream. It also obliterates the notion of class struggle because in a society partitioned by cognitive ability, there is no possibility of full justice or equality. What there is, is a crude, brutal, social reality dictated by biological determinism mixed with elitism.

For the Left elite to tackle these issues, they would have had to transform their entire philosophical and methodological structure. They'd have had to give up on dogmatism and sound-bites, and proceed into an ethical thinking that is dynamically flexible and unpredictable. This was never going to happen. But most importantly, to address the issues raised by Herrnstein and Murray, the Left would have had to attach itself to reality, to open its eyes and see the millions of struggling Americans, to empathize with their struggle rather than insulting them. This wasn't going to happen either. Facing reality defies the nature of Left, liberal and progressive thinking. Looking at the world as it is just interferes with the fantasy, that endless empty talk about progressive and liberal values. It's always been easier to just burn books.

The New Left, the Liberals and the progressives were successful in their efforts to critically burn *The Bell Curve*, but failed to defeat its message – as tens of millions of impoverished Americans can attest. Those who tried to silence those devastating predictions from 1994 woke up on November 9th 2016 to find out that the impoverished blue-collar Americans had elected Donald Trump to be their president.

The book and its message could have alerted Americans to their emerging dystopia, but instead it was reduced into a ferocious battle between a few Jewish academics. Stephen J Gould and Noam Chomsky on one side and Richard J. Herrnstein on the other. As we will now see, this was no coincidence as America was left to its fate.

The Final Piece in the Jigsaw

"The best way to control the opposition is to lead it ourselves." A quote attributed to Vladimir Ilych Lenin[100]

Throughout modern history, various Jewish agitators have agreed that something is quintessentially wrong with Jewry. Repeatedly, these rebels have seen that something intrinsically associated with the Jews, their culture or politics at various times, has become a 'Jewish problem.'

Early Zionism was such a phase in Jewish history. The early Zionists agreed with the so-called anti-Semites about the 'parasitic nature' of the Jewish diaspora and determined to cure these 'problematic Jewish symptoms' by means of a 'homecoming' – a 'resettlement' in Zion (Palestine). They vowed to take the Jews away and make them into a productive nation and a 'people like all other people.'

Contemporary Jewish anti-Zionists have also reached an

---

100. It is worth mentioning that although the above quote is often attributed to Lenin, I didn't manage to identify the source.

agreement amongst themselves that 'Zionism' and the 'Israeli occupation' have become a 'Jewish problem.' They oppose the occupation – the continuing sovereignty over the territories obtained by Israel in 1967 in the name of their own Jewishness, and in line with vaguely-defined universal Jewish ethics.

Likewise, Karl Marx thought capitalism was a 'Jewish problem.' In his article, *On the Jewish Question*, he contended that in order for the world to liberate itself from capitalism, it had better emancipate itself from the Jews.[101]

So, it seems that, at times and repeatedly, Jewish dissenters and intellectuals agree with the Goyim and the anti-Semites that something is wrong with the Jews, or at least with some Jews.

Figure K

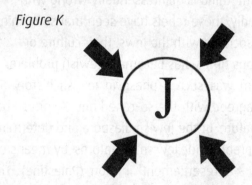

---

101 ."What is the secular basis of Judaism? *Practical* need, *self-interest*. What is the worldly religion of the Jew? *Huckstering*. What is his worldly God? *Money*. Very well then! Emancipation from huckstering and money, consequently from practical, real Judaism, would be the self-emancipation of our time." Karl Marx *On The Jewish Question*, 1844

In Figure K, the encircled J stands for 'a problem attributed to the Jews' – an awkward trait or a something troubling associated with Jewry. The arrows symbolize growing public unease and opposition to that 'problem.'

Modern Jewish history indicates that many things can become a 'Jewish problem': Palestine, banking, Wall Street, neocon wars, ID politics, cultural Marxism, cultural hegemony within Hollywood and the media – are just some of the explosive topics that have been associated with the Jews, their culture and power.

Typically, Jews use different measures such as legislation and political correctness to stifle discussion of such topics and the roles of Jews within them, but sporadically a few ethically-awakened Jews will see the problem and openly proclaim their dissent from the dominant Jewish narrative. They often do so because they believe that such opposition to their brethren is good for their community, i.e., they insist that the particular 'Jewish problem' (AIPAC, Palestine, capitalism etc.) reflects badly on the Jews as a whole so they, 'as Jews,' must speak out.

This is the basis for the emergence of a marginal satellite discourse of Jewish dissent, as depicted in Figure L:

Figure L

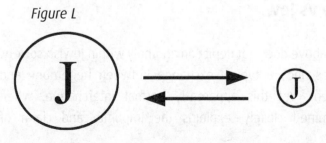

The satellite dissent discourse represented by the little encircled J (on the right) is formed to criticize the Jewish dominant discourse as a 'Jewish problem' (big J on the Left).

The emergence of dissent within the Jewish discourse is usually followed (Figure M) by a lively and often virulent internal exchange between the hegemonic Jewish rhetoric (left) and the marginal satellite dissenters (right).

Figure M

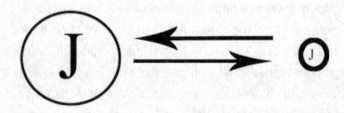

It is important to emphasize that the emergence of this Jewish satellite dissent is not necessarily conspiratorial. The dissent is often genuine and authentic; indeed, it is entirely rational for an ethical person of Jewish origin to feel uneasy about Israeli crimes, financial disasters associated with Jewish bankers, Zionist/Neocon wars etc.

Jew vs Jew

The above does not depict an anomaly within Jewish society. It describes a typical exchange between hegemony and dissent. Yet this apparently normal interchange, when examined closely, explains the impunity and claim of omnipotence that are intrinsic to Jewish politics. The following will illustrate the unique dynamic relationship between the Jews and 'the rest.'

Once those elements among the general public who were initially upset, disturbed or even outraged by a given 'Jewish problem' (Figure K) become aware of an emerging Jewish dissent, they tend to back off. They let the Jews fight amongst themselves. In practice, the appearance of an internal Jewish debate leads to the suspension of general opposition to the 'Jewish problem.' Those who were initially disturbed by a 'Jewish problem' form a new theatre set on the perimeter (Figure N) of the discourse. They consciously remove themselves from the debate (the inverted arrows); they come to regard the topic as an internal Jewish affair.

Figure N

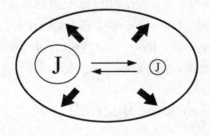

This unique dynamic explains the Jewish domination of, say, the Palestinian solidarity discourse. Palestine solidarity is now an internal Jewish affair with Palestinians alienated and estranged from the discussion about their own liberation. The same applies to opposition to neocon politics where a few Zionist Jews have positioned themselves as the final authorities on the interventionist wars and the current philosophical debate has been reduced to an internal Zionist pseudo-ethical quibble between neocon Sam Harris and light Zionist Noam Chomsky.

Similarly, in May 2015 there was controversy following ultra-Zionist Pamela Geller's Mohammad-drawing cartoon contest in Texas, when Geller's event was attacked by two Muslim gunmen. Even America's most conservative and right-wing media expressed outrage at Geller's anti-Muslim attitude[102] and, in a matter of hours, Pamela Geller, a popular Zionist celebrity, had become a 'Jewish problem.' In less than a day, full-on Jewish dissent to Pamela Geller had formed but this time it wasn't the Jewish left who opposed the Zionist bigot: the thrust of the opposition came from ultra-Zionist Abe Foxman and his notorious ADL. As the discussion above would predict, the American media backed off leaving the debate on Geller's Islamophobia to Foxman and his female Zionist twin, Pamela Geller. Geller's contest and its repercussions were no longer an American problem, it became an 'internal Jewish affair.'

Alt-Right or Talmudic Quarrel?

The suppression of dissent and control of the opposition are not exclusively Left tactics. It is prominent within Right American circles and especially the American Alt-Right.

---

102. http://therightscoop.com/chris-matthews-pamela-geller-caused-texas-shooting-by-setting-a-trap-for-muslims-compares-to-nazis/

In 2003, the Southern Law Poverty Centre (SLPC), detected a growing right wing interest in the Frankfurt School, Wilhelm Reich and the Jewish intelligentsia's role in the creation of that school of thought. The SLPC grasped that cultural Marxism and its legacy was about to become the 'next Jewish problem.' In a preemptive attack, Bill Berkowitz wrote in SLPC's magazine *Intelligence Report*, "Right-wing ideologues, racists and other extremists have jazzed up political correctness and repackaged it – in its most virulent form, as an anti-Semitic theory that identifies Jews in general and several Jewish intellectuals in particular as nefarious, communistic destroyers. These supposed originators of 'cultural Marxism' are seen as conspiratorial plotters intent on making Americans feel guilty and thus subverting their Christian culture."[103]

I guess that Berkowitz didn't bother to look into the history of the Frankfurt School and neo-Marxists and find out for himself what Reich, Adorno, Marcuse, Horkheimer, Fromm and others within this milieu believed in, or stood for. Berkowitz continues, "in a nutshell, the theory posits that a tiny group of Jewish philosophers who fled Germany in the 1930s and set up shop at Columbia University in New York City devised an unorthodox form of 'Marxism' that took aim at American society's culture, rather than its economic system. The theory holds that these self-interested Jews — the so-called Frankfurt School of philosophers — planned to try to convince mainstream Americans that white ethnic

---

103. *Cultural Marxism Catching On*, Bill Berkowitz, SLPC, August 15, 2003

pride is bad, that sexual liberation is good, and that supposedly traditional American values — Christianity, family values, and so on — are reactionary and bigoted. With their core values thus subverted, the theory goes, Americans would be quick to sign on to the ideas of the far left."[104]

Berkowitz and the SPLC had a good reason to fear that cultural Marxism was about to become the 'new Jewish problem.' They could see that the opposition to these influential progressive schools of thoughts were open to being led by American conservatives and patriots – people who were not necessarily Jewish or identified politically and culturally as Jews. Berkowitz was certainly aware of the invaluable work of Kevin MacDonald, particularly his 1998 work, *The Culture of Critique*. Here, MacDonald, an evolutionary psychologist, studied the intellectual evolution of the Frankfurt School within the context of Jewish survival strategy. Berkowitz was also aware of long-time Washington conservative Pat Buchanan's disgust with cultural Marxism. Yet, neither MacDonald nor Buchanan's eloquent and precise opposition to Identitarian politics matured into any popular opposition. But the sharp rise in grassroots patriotic and anti-Identitarian politics in the US may have provided the hint that, as in so many times before, it was time to grab control of the opposition and, as expected, by 2010 cultural Marxism had become a 'Jewish problem.'

The most popular contemporary American critic of cultural Marxism was Andrew Breitbart, the right-wing founder of the widely-read news blog, breitbart.com. Andrew Breitbart, a

---

104. Ibid

successful journalist, was critical of all forms of ID politics as well as of the tyranny of correctness. He specifically deconstructed the work of the leading Frankfurt School thinkers and, from a conservative perspective, analysed their corrosive impact on American society.

Andrew Breitbart died in 2012 (43) soon after he published his best-selling book, *Righteous Indignation: Excuse Me While I Save the World!*, which amongst other things, comprehensively deconstructed cultural Marxism and the Frankfurt School. Breitbart was the shooting star of the Alt-Right, the intellectual face of the Tea Party and the foremost critic of the Frankfurt School's attempt to subvert American society. But it is worth mentioning that Breitbart never missed an opportunity to mention his Jewish upbringing and the significant impact on him of his *barmitzvah* training.

Andrew Breitbart's criticism of the Frankfurt School wasn't only valid and intellectually principled, it was also a good read. Breitbart was a great writer. He delivered the most horrific message in the most personal manner and all peppered with dark humour. He understood the cultural Marxist project. He grasped its tyrannical and ideological nature. In reference to Marcuse's concept of 'Repressive Tolerance' Breitbart wrote, "the First Amendment – the same instrument that allowed the Frankfurt School to land on our shores and express their pernicious idea in freedom – was now curtailed by those who had benefitted from it."[105]

---

105. *Righteous Indignation: Excuse Me While I Save the World*, Andrew Breitbart, (2012) pg 122

But understandably, Breitbart was reluctant to point out the Jewish orientation at the core of cultural Marxism and the Frankfurt School, in fact, he avoided the topic completely. For Andrew Breitbart, the writers Adorno, Fromm, Marcuse, Reich, and Horkeheimer were "just Germans[106] who came to America and interfered with our Judeo-Christian values." It was a pretty sophisticated spin – to turn the Frankfurt School into ordinary Germans and, at the same time, to turn Americans into Jews.

So, Americans were now 'Judeo-Christians', but what are those Judeo-Christian values that the evil cultural Marxist was so committed to suppress or even to obliterate? Are these precepts real, or are they a political construct, or perhaps just a myth? And is it really a coincidence that Breitbart, while working hard to graft the 'Judeo' onto Christian universal values, failed to notice the Jewish secularist origins of the cultural Marxist project?

The meaning of the Judeo-Christian canon to which Breitbart refers is vague and obscure. It is true that Christianity and Judaism share some scriptures but the history of the relationship between the Jewish and the Christian is not one of hyphenated harmony, but one of continuous animosity and even some genocides. Zionism came to life in the late 19th century because Jewish intellectuals such as Herzl, Nordau and Jabotinsky came to the conclusion that Jews and Christians had little in common and had better be separated once and for all.

---

106. Wilhelm Reich was actually Austrian.

Yet Americans love to believe that their nation is founded on these supposedly shared tenets, and it is true that the American founding fathers were attached to the Old Testament and the Ten Commandments. The trouble is that, while it's pretty clear what the Christian founding fathers took from the scriptures, it is less clear what the so-called 'Judeo' part brought to the deal.

Some insist that these Judeo-Christian values stretch back to the Declaration of Independence: "We hold these truths to be self-evident, that all men are created equal, that they are endowed by their Creator with certain unalienable rights, that among these are life, liberty and the pursuit of happiness..." But those who believe that this is an embodiment of Judeo-Christian thinking may also have to explain why such liberal attitudes are so foreign to Judaic thinking. In Judaic thinking, most men may well be created equal, but some are born chosen. In short, those universal attitudes, fundamental to Christianity and Islam, are totally alien to the tribal core of Judaism.

I believe that this notion of 'Judeo-Christian values' was re-popularised after 9/11 to create an imaginary spiritual alliance between Zionism, Israel and American imperialism, after which we heard a widespread call for a global war against the Arab and Muslim world. 'Judeo-Christian values' have become just another pretext for more and more Israeli-encouraged wars.

I now believe that Andrew Breitbart criticising Cultural Marxists in the name of this canonical construct was a sophisticated attempt to conceal the simple fact that the

Cultural Marxists had declared a war against Christianity, the Church and Christian values. It certainly wasn't the 'Judeo' that the Cultural Marxists fought.

Now, the debate is obscured by both sides. Now, the most crucial American debate of our times, a debate about the very meaning of freedom, the nature of political exchange and the prospects for society has been reduced, once again, to an internal Jewish dispute. On the one hand, the Left-Zionist-leaning Southern Law Poverty Centre bars any attempt to look into the origins of cultural Marxism, and, on the other hand, Breitbart and other Breitbarters accuse cultural Marxism of interfering with 'Judeo-Christian' values while concealing that cultural Marxism is, amongst other things, a (secular) Judeo-progressive assault on Christians, Christianity, and the Church, as well as on American nationalism and rootedness.

Breitbart wasn't the only popular Jewish critic of cultural Marxism. David Horowitz, a conservative, ultra-Zionist agitator, was among the first Americans to attack Cultural Marxism. Young Horowitz was raised in the 1950s as a Jewish American Communist and evolved into an ardent New Left enthusiast (1960s) and an advocate of ID politics. So, when he morphed into an enemy of the Left (1970s), he was well positioned to grasp what he was up against.

Conservative blogger Lee Stranahan commented on his own political website, leestranahan.com, on the significant role of the Jews in the fight against cultural Marxism. "It's equally true that the major figures at the Frankfurt School were all Jewish and also that some of the major figures exposing the Frankfurt School such as Andrew Breitbart and

David Horowitz are also Jewish."[107] For the gentile Stranahan, it is safer to allow the Jewish Andrew Breitbart and David Horowitz take care of what he clearly sees as a 'Jewish problem,' for at least no one can accuse them of being anti-Semitic. And by now, you will be less surprised when some Palestinian supporters use precisely the same argument; that leaving it to Jews to lead the battle against the Jewish state is a safe strategy. And, indeed, it is safe because it leads nowhere.

The current star of the Alt-Right and a fierce enemy of Identitarian politics is the conservative 'gay Catholic' Milo Yiannopoulos, who has successfully transformed satellite, dissident tactics into an art form. Most of the time, Yiannopoulos is Catholic, but, when occasion demands, he transforms himself into a proud Jew. In an Internet TV interview with Dave Rubin, Yiannopoulos said, "The alt-right people, the people who like me, they're not anti-Semites. They don't care about Jews. I mean, they may have some assumptions about things, how the Jews run everything; well, we do. How the Jews run the banks; well, we do. How the Jews run the media; well, we do. They're right about all that stuff. ... It's a fact, this is not in debate. It's a statistical fact ... Jews are vastly disproportionately represented in all of these professions. It's just a fact. It's not anti-Semitic to point out statistics."[108] Yiannopoulos' effortless shift from Catholic to proud Jew

107. Lee Stranahan - *Duping The Idiots: The Left's Frankfurt School Denialism*, Sept. 18, 2013

108. http://www.tabletmag.com/jewish-news-and-politics/203888/donald-trumps-little-boy

exemplifies a state of affairs where pretty much every crucial political and cultural battle is transformed into an albeit highly entertaining, Jewish squabble which, for practical purposes, will simply chase its own tail.

But in case it wasn't already clear where Breitbart's loyalties rest, President Donald Trump's appointment of former Breitbart News chairman Stephen K. Bannon as his chief strategist and senior counsellor provided for us a window into the proximity between Zionism and the leading American Alt-Right outlet.

On appointment by Trump, Bannon was immediately accused by most American mainstream and Jewish outlets of being "a raging anti-Semite" and a "white supremacist." In the *New York Daily News*, Shaun King insisted that "Donald Trump is using Stephen Bannon to turn the GOP into the new KKK,"[109] and the ADL's CEO Jonathan Greenblatt used the most severe language in reaction to Bannon's appointment: "It is a sad day when a man who presided over the premier website of the 'alt-right' — a loose-knit group of white nationalists and unabashed anti-Semites and racists — is slated to be a senior staff member in the 'people's house"[110].

Surprise? It took less than one day before we learned that Bannon is actually pro-Semitic and an ardent supporter of Israel and Zionism.

Ben Shapiro who left Breitbart News after a falling out with Bannon wrote, "I have no evidence that Bannon's a racist or

---

109. https://t.co/1i3ettRdMb

110. http://www.latimes.com/nation/politics/trailguide/la-na-trailguide-updates-what-is-the-alt-right-a-refresher-1479169663-htmlstory.html

that he's an anti-Semite."[111] The notorious Zionist Alan Dershowitz followed the same line, arguing that it is "not legitimate to call somebody an anti-Semite because you might disagree with their policies."[112] The ultra-Zionist David Horowitz, added his voice, insisting that the accusations against Bannon were completely without foundation and Joel Pollack, Breitbart staff writer, also an Orthodox Jew, informed us that Steve Bannon is actually "a friend of the Jewish people and a defender of Israel ... if anything, he is overly sensitive about it, and often takes offense on Jews' behalf."[113]

So, Brietbart, the leading right-wing intellectual outlet, is infested with Zionists and Zionists supporters. This shouldn't take us by surprise, since we know that Zionism is a right-wing ideology that subscribes to racism, nationalism and patriotism. But for the American people the implications could be devastating since the most crucial American political debate of our times now seems to be an internal Jewish exchange.

Symbiosis

The Goy has good reason to remove himself from direct conflict with the Jew. He prefers to let the Jews fight it out

---

111. http://www.dailywire.com/news/10770/3-thoughts-steve-bannon-white-house-chief-ben-shapiro

112. http://www.breitbart.com/jerusalem/2016/11/15/alan-dershowitz-steve-bannon-smears-not-legitimate-call-somebody-anti-semite-disagree-policies/

113. http://www.breitbart.com/big-government/2016/11/14/stephen-k-bannon-friend-jewish-people-defender-israel/§

amongst themselves. The gentile understands that a conflict with the Jew can lead to tragic consequences. It has the potential to make the Shoah into a frequent occurrence – clearly, not an ideal scenario for either the gentile or the Jew. Both Jews and gentiles prefer to avoid the outbreak of violence. The internal dynamic created by Jewish satellite dissent facilitates the deferral of such outbreaks.

The table below juxtaposes 'Jewish problems' with the corresponding marginal, Jewish satellite dissent. The table illuminates how the satellite opposition tackles and effectively dilutes those complications associated with perceived troublesome Jewish symptoms.

Jewish 'Problems'	Jewish Satellite Dissent
Capitalism: Banking, Wall Street, money, Goldman Sachs, Rothschild, Bernays	The Left: Karl Marx, Jewish Left, Trotsky, Rosa Luxemburg, Early Zionists, Labour Zionism, The Bund etc.
Zionist politics and lobbying: AIPAC, Sheldon Adelson, Haim Saban	Dissident Jewish Lobby: J-Street, George Soros, Occupy AIPAC
Palestine and Israeli brutality	Peace Now, B'Tselem, Yesh Gvul, *Mondoweiss*, JVP, IJAN
Liberal values: Cultural Marxism, Frankfurt School, Political Correctness, New Left, advocacy of Immigration, ID politics & LGBT	Andrew Breitbart, Milo Yiannopoulos, David Horowitz, Breitbart.com, Alain Finkielkraut, Melanie Phillips

Pro War Neocon Ideology: Zionist Wars, Sam Harris	Anti War: *Democracy Now*-Amy Goodman, Noam Chomsky
Media domination	Alternative Media: *Democracy Now*, Paul Jay & *Real News*
Jewish Islamophobia: Pamela Geller	ADL, Abe Foxman, Southern Poverty Law Centre
Holocaust Religion and Shoah orthodoxy	Holocaust revisionism: David Cole, Yeshayahu Leibowitz, Paul Eisen, Hanna Yablonka[114]

The Rise of Perspectives

Let's look back on some of the great events of post-WWII history - the battle between Left and Right, and the cold war, the formation of the Jewish state followed by the expulsion of the Palestinians and the beginning of the Israeli Arab conflict, the neocon wars, the 2008 credit-crunch, and so on.

While those events were happening, few of us were able to grasp their true relevance or significant meaning. It is only when historical perspective comes into play that we can revisit and possibly revise our understanding of our past.

Looking back at the Left/Right dispute with historical perspective, we may discover that what at the time seemed

114. To read more: Education Ministry Bumps Professor From Post for Criticizing 'Superficial' Teaching of Holocaust, Haaretz, Jul 21, 2010 http://www.haaretz.com/education-ministry-bumps-professor-from-post-for-criticizing-superficial-teaching-of-holocaust-1.303097

an earth-shattering struggle was in fact a relatively minor feud between a few bankers and some cultural Marxists. At the end of the day, the ideological and spiritual distance between the Frankfurt School cultural Marxists and Alisa Zinov'yevna Rosenbaum (Ayn Rand) may not be as wide as we thought – and the same may apply to liberal George Soros and the hundreds of progressive organizations funded by his Open Society Institute. In short, capitalism and the New Left may be just two sides of the same coin.

The Palestinian conflict also has been reduced to an internal Jewish dispute between some ultra-Zionist politicians and commentators, and some Jewish anti-Zionists (Mondoweiss, JVP, IJAN) who claim to empathize 'equally' with the Palestinians and the Israelis, as if the oppressor and the oppressed were equal.

When debating neocon Zionist wars, clearly now a global disaster with no prospect of solution, we are left with a pseudo-intellectual feud between Sam Harris and Noam Chomsky. Would you trust the Alt-Right's Andrew Breitbart, David Horowitz or Milo Yiannopoulos to dismantle Cultural Marxism on your behalf? I don't.

Finally, the academy award winning film *Inside Job* shows the 2008 crash as an argument between George Soros and Dominique Strauss Khan on the one hand, and Alan Greenspan and his friends at Goldman Sachs and Lehman Brothers on the other. I guess that this is the true depiction of our current disaster.

A close look at our recent past may suggest that what we saw as titanic ideological struggles, were, in reality, internal disputes between people who are, on the things that really matter, pretty much in agreement. Such a revelation is surely devastating to any notion of democracy, free speech and fundamental fairness.

Consider the millions of lives wasted and impoverished by these conflicts and crises, and then surely our failure to think in a true ethical or even historical way is, to say the least, troublesome. We saw the same devastating realisations occur in Europe in the 1930s with well-documented dire consequences and yet we may be allowing the same to happen again, with similar devastating results.

Throughout this book I have asked some questions. When did it go wrong? When did the liberal promise disappear? Why did our grand political theories fail? How is it possible that Western academia and media failed to understand or explain such profound changes? I hope we are now ready to tackle these questions.

In the so-called post-political condition in which we live, little is shared between the political and the human, in effect between politics and people. This does not mean that nothing takes place in politics which affects people, but it does mean that we, the people, have been unable to influence matters or even express our wishes. We've spent most of our time enjoying the show, chewing popcorn while Donald and Hillary hit each other below the belt, mere spectators in a Greek tragedy that just happens to be the story of our destruction. But in effect, 'after politics' is a tale of the complete victory by one oligarchy. The consequences may be fatal for our planet.

The Fatal Continuum

Imagine your child is ill. He has missed nursery school for a few days but, for the moment, you're not too concerned. But as the situation continues you decide to visit the GP, who diagnoses the problem that seems plausible and prescribes a course of action that you are happy to follow.

But the situation continues to deteriorate and your child finds it hard to breathe. Now, you rush the boy or girl to the hospital, to be examined by three consultants who, to your disquiet, agree on a different diagnosis and treatment. You follow the new regime, but your child's health still deteriorates, but you don't give up. You take your child from city to city, you cross oceans and visit clinics in every capital, but to no avail. It seems that not a single doctor can save your child. You struggle and manage to sustain your child's life for a few more years but eventually organs fail, eyesight diminishes, paralysis sets in, and then death.

Old and exhausted, after so many terrible years, you stand at your child's funeral. You are beside yourself with grief and can hardly think straight. But then, you notice a bunch of people who look familiar. Some seem to be as old as you and some seem older. They appear to be distressed and seem to share your pain, they come over to you, they shake your hand and offer condolences. You've seen them before, but you can't recall when or where. Then a voice whispers into your ear, "Can you not see what is going on here? Did you really fail to notice all those years the connection between your child's illness and all these doctors who purported to help you?" Finally you understand – the illness and the doctors are one; intrinsically bonded, bound together, two sides of the same coin.

This allegory could refer to the Israeli-Palestinian conflict. If the sick child with the mysterious disease is the Jewish state and all the doctors are the Jewish 'specialists' such as Ilan Pappe, Jeff Halper, Noam Chomsky, Zochrot, Shlomo Sand, JVP, Max Blumenthal, Miko Peled, Norman Finkelstein, Mondoweiss, Israel Shahak and even myself, then for seventy years we have allowed Jewish political consultants to (mis)diagnose and treat a 'Jewish disease', a disease which lies at the heart of the Zionist project. And then we are surprised that we have failed to cure our poor, sick Palestinian 'child' whom we loved so much?

And it's not just Palestine. If Marx was right and capitalism is a Jewish symptom, is it any surprise that, with our other herd of Jewish revolutionary theoretical GPs (Marx, Trotsky, Rosa Luxemburg, Wilhelm Reich, Adorno, Marcuse, The Frankfurt School etc.), we have failed to find a remedy?

And what about the neo-con wars, that shift from the Zionist promised land to the neo-con promised planet? Can we really expect Drs. Noam Chomsky, Amy Goodman and George Soros to identify the disease and find the cure?

If, as I believe it is, cultural Marxism is a Jewish problem then the 'doctors' to whom we look for a solution need, in themselves to be pretty distinct and distant from the problem. And right now, as you read these words, can Milo Yiannopoulos, Breitbart.com, David Horowitz, or Ben Shapiro save the people of Michigan from the virulent disease spread by a few Wall Street Mammonites? Can they save America?

In this book, I have shone a light into the matrix of controlled opposition and it is clear to me that creating and maintaining dissent in order to control opposition is deeply embedded in modern, Jewish, secular politics. And yet, I still believe that, in most cases, it is not intentionally inspired. There are no conspiracies here. Chomsky, Goodman, Adorno and Breitbart are not necessarily consciously deceiving us; indeed, they may well be doing their best, within the context of a limited tribal mindset. The truth is, they cannot think out of the box, they cannot climb over the ghetto walls that enclose their own tribal beings.

But can the same not be said of the rest of us? Do we not also limit ourselves to the boundaries of political correctness? Do we not, once we have decided that it's okay because the Jews will take care of it themselves, also disengage ourselves from any discussion of any 'Jewish problem?'

"The best way to control the opposition is to lead it ourselves," was Lenin's subversive political insight and Orwell's 1984 provided a fictionalized example of a political apparatus in which this insight is put into practice. As the tyranny of correctness dismantles our ability to think, create and oppose, critical thinking is suppressed. In 1984 the tyranny of correctness restricts the discourse and stops the people from seeing that Emmanuel Goldstein is not really the 'enemy of the state,' but that he, himself, is a symptom of the disease. And isn't it correctness, pure and simple, that stops us from ever mentioning the fact that the protagonist Goldstein is, himself, Jewish?

However much seeing Emmanuel Goldstein in everyone and everything may seem paranoid, within our post-political condition, such fear is entirely rational. Our 'oppositions' are always delusional and Emmanuel Goldstein is everyone, everywhere and everything – ourselves included.

Introduction

"In art, self-exploration is exploration of the world"
-Otto Weininger: Sex & Character, 2003 pg ix.

It's unusual to put one's introduction at the end of a text. However, I like to think that every end is also a new beginning – if it were not, the act of writing this book would only defeat itself.

We live in an era of science and technology, accepting that scientific innovations are the key to our survival and technology makes life sustainable, efficient and most importantly, convenient. Within this scientific-technological realm, man is the master of the universe. Man is the observer, the universe is the observed, man is the subject, the world at his feet is but a compendium of objects. The 'master' uses the objects at his disposal (technology) and sets the objects so they fit nicely within his theories and models (science).

An adherence to such subject/object dichotomy leads to detachment. Most of us are alienated even from our own bodies. We see our survival in terms of metabolic chains connected to each other. Similarly, our socio-political environment is reduced to statistics, algorithms, demography, and socioeconomic classes. Even psychology has become a Pandora's Box, with the contents kinetically kick-started by varied personality complexes that are somehow attached to us by structured models.

This book isn't like that. This book is sorely lacking in scientific content. It provides no statistics, empirical studies or even test cases. In my work, it is us – you and me – who are the facts. We are the test cases. For me, inquiry is a never-ending self-examination. As Otto Weininger notes above, I contend that self-exploration is exploration of the world.

Questions such as 'what is beauty?' or 'what can we know?' aspire to re-unite our human faculties. The validity of our answers to these questions is measured by means of self-reflection. It is this fundamental unity which is the basis of Athenian thought and which has been brutally suppressed. This must change. Pythagoras, Kant and Heidegger didn't need statistics or microscopes and neither do we.

My readers often tell me that my thoughts are not new to them; 'you have managed to articulate what I knew all along' they sometimes say. To me, this makes perfect sense. Philosophy can be summed up, as Martin Heidegger put it, as a prolonged story of 'forgetfulness of Being', the story of that which is closest to us and yet most mysterious and unattainable. Being and time are like the tip of your nose, so close you fail to see it. The truth is there at all times, all we have to do is open our eyes and contemplate it.

I speak here about a return to Athens.

Glossary

AIPAC - The American Israel Public Affairs Committee, American Jewish Lobby Group

BDS – The call to boycott, divest and sanction Israel

CFI – Conservative Friends of Israel, British Jewish lobby group

CRIF - Council of Representatives of French Jews, French Jewish Lobby Group

Cultural Marxism – also known as Critical Theory is a collection of neo Marxist political theories that focus on cultural factors as agents for social change

Goy, Goyim - The Yiddish label for gentile, gentiles

ID Politics – Identity Politics

JVP – Jewish Voice for Peace

Mammon - the Hebrew biblical word for wealth

Mammonism - the seeking of mammon for the sake of Mammon

Tikkun Olam - the (unfounded) belief that the Jews posses knowledge of how to make the world a better place